*To angie
love
michelle*

PRAISE FOR **APPOINTED**

Any woman struggling with insignificance will benefit greatly from reading *Appointed*! Autumn shares from an authentic heart how women can choose victory over defeat, regardless of the challenges and heartaches in life. Autumn inspires and encourages women to look to the truth found in Scripture to define them, instead of the lies that keep women back from knowing their purpose in life. You don't want to miss out on this timely read!

DR. MONICA ROSE BRENNAN
Author and Speaker
Associate Professor, Women's Ministries, Liberty University

Autumn Miles's passion to see future generations equipped to walk in purpose is a force that is palpable and contagious. Her life is evidence of a God who redeems and a truth that will set people free.

HARMONY DUST
Founder, Treasures Ministries
Author, *Scars and Stilettos*

As a pastor, I see the need for women to recognize their appointed purpose. In the book *Appointed*, Autumn Miles addresses this timely topic from a refreshing biblical perspective. I recommend this volume for anyone needing hope in this area of her life.

DR. ROBERT JEFFRESS
Senior Pastor, First Baptist Church Dallas

Autumn Miles is a living example of someone who has emerged as a successful and powerful person, despite challenging circumstances. This book is for anyone who may be struggling with finding freedom in her life. Autumn's honest, tenacious and tell-it-like-it-is approach will help countless individuals find hope through Scripture and practical application. Thank you, Autumn, for using your voice and sharing your personal story . . . you are a champion!

CHERYL LUKE
Writer and Speaker
Women's Pastor, Shoreline Church, Austin, Texas

Autumn Miles is a brilliant, sought-after and dynamic communicator. This book is a real, raw and candid look at Autumn's journey from navigating a painful past to emerging into one of the voices of this generation. From learning the importance of praying as if your life depended on it, to facing the future with a strong conviction of vision and faith, this book will remind you that great is *His* faithfulness. You will see your story in her story as she beautifully leads you to the cross through her freedom found in knowing Christ.

EARL AND ONEKA MCCLELLEN
Pastors, Shoreline Dallas

Autumn Miles is passionate about helping women see themselves as God does. In her book *Appointed*, she uses her own life experiences to connect on a personal level. *Appointed* is a heartfelt, eloquent and honest book that will both excite and challenge the reader. This inspirational message of hope is a must read for women of all ages!

CLINT NOWERY
Middle School Director, Browns Bridge Community Church (North Point Ministries)

Autumn's passion for Scripture, prayer and a deep desire to see the Holy Spirit alive in this generation pierces through her writing. Her transparent experiences of hardship and breakthrough, will encourage you as you see God's story alive in her!

BRIAN WURZELL
Worship Pastor, Hillside Community Church, Rancho Cucamonga, California

APPOINTED

THE PAST IS THE PAST

your future starts now

Autumn Miles

Revell

a division of Baker Publishing Group

Grand Rapids, Michigan

Published by Revell
A division of Baker Publishing Group
P.O. Box 6287, Grand Rapids, MI 49516-6287
www.revellbooks.com

Printed in the United States of America

Library of Congress Cataloging-in-Publication Data is on file at the Library of Congress, Washington, DC.

14 15 16 17 18 19 20 | 7 6 5 4 3 2

This book is dedicated to my God and Father.
Without Your love and forgiveness, I would not be able to truly live.
Thank You for being the Redeemer of my past and
the holder of my future. My life is Yours.
Use this book and the words in it to show whoever reads it
that You are King.

CONTENTS

Introduction

I was addicted to getting attention until I was 18. "Anything for attention" was my secret motto. I thrived on shock value. My dad was a pastor in Indiana. When I found out that some people in the church didn't approve of my being a cheerleader, I was determined to be the best cheerleader I could be. I spent my teen years eating weird things and saying offensive things to tickle this need to be somebody. If I was playing a game of truth or dare, I wouldn't dream of choosing truth. Dare was the theme of my life, and I wore it well. Although I was a Christian, I knew Satan wanted to steal my influence for Christ, and on many occasions, I obliged.

My way brought me to the point of lying on the floor of my small house, married to a man who hated me, begging God for help. My quest to live a life of man-made significance had miserably failed, and now I battled a fate I had carved out for myself years earlier. In my insecurity, I thought I needed to create significance for myself when all the while God had already made me significant.

On my most desperate day, more than a decade ago, my significance became a reality to me when I surrendered my way to God and understood that He had accepted me all along. My life drastically changed for the better. When all the attention from others faded, and I was completely alone, God was there. He never left. He was waiting for me. In that moment, I became an ex-nobody.

My life has never been the same. My heart changed so drastically that day that I began to feel sorry for the girl I had been for so many years. I also began my journey of wanting to use my life, and the gifts God has entrusted to me, to help other young women.

Here's the deal: We all want significance. It's that burning desire inside of you to be noticed or accepted. Some of us, including me, have gone to great lengths to try to achieve a life we think we need. We, as young women, continue to buy a lie. Satan tells us that we need to add something to ourselves to be significant, such as a guy or a ton of money. But God tells us the opposite. He clearly tells us that we have purpose from the time of our conception

1

The Significance of You

I wish that I was [making a difference], and there are days that I feel that I am, but I'm not 100 percent of that purpose right now. The world could exist without me, maybe not even noticing that I was gone.

BLUSH ATTENDEE

**Do you believe that the world could exist without you—
that your life makes a difference no matter what you are feeling?**

It was a beautiful fall Sunday morning in a small town in Indiana. There was a time in my life when I had loved the morning. I used to love waking up to get ready for whatever was going to greet me that day. Those years seemed like a distant memory as my husband and I backed out of the garage to head to church. My heart sank when I noticed that something was clinging to the car. I knew there would be hell to pay if I had anything to do with it.

It was around the time of Halloween, and I could see that the colorful leaves on our trees had been decorated in brilliant white garlands of toilet paper. We had been the victims of a good old-fashioned toilet-papering prank. What most people would see as good fun was a major event in our life. My husband's frustration immediately ramped up as he tried to figure out why someone would TP our house and, more important to him, who did it. I sat in silence as we drove to church. I knew that any comment from me would be attacked.

I felt petrified with dread during church service as I thought about the repercussions this incident would have on me for the rest of the day. It would be a long afternoon. When we arrived home, I immediately went for the broom and silently started to clean up the mess. He came out of the house and began working, but it wasn't long before he began to verbally strip me of any sense of worth. All I can remember were the words "You are f*$@ing stupid," repeated over and over. Those words cut like a knife, and I just stood there and took it. My body ached while I swept the porch of my little 1,200-square-foot house. I am not sure of the medical term when you hurt so bad emotionally that you hurt physically, and it doesn't matter. That day, I had given up hope of ever being significant, and the tears streamed down my face.

Let's Get Real

Are you at all familiar with that kind of scenario? Have you given up hope of ever feeling like an individual who will leave a legacy of significance? There are many reasons why people bury their significance. They stand at their own wake, forfeiting what could have been. Feelings of inadequacy, trials, betrayal, mistakes, lies, lack of resources—any or all can brainwash you into believing that you were simply created to exist, and nothing more.

I understand. When my hope died, so did my future. My sense of self lay dormant for a time, and I gave in to the death of my significance. Today, I want to challenge your thinking, sweet friend. The key to living a life filled with significance is to choose to believe what God has written about you in His Word. Many will say that they believe the Bible and the teaching therein, but they don't. How do I know that? Their lives don't reflect any excitement for Christ. They don't truly believe; they have merely retained the information of what the Word says.

Belief means living as if the Bible is fact. If our Christian culture believed that the Bible was fact—every living, breathing part of it—the news media would be clogged with stories of the miraculous performed by Christians through the power of God. There would be no stereotype of a Christian as someone who doesn't tip food servers on Sunday, or someone who is bound to legalism and rules.

Radical, heroic and impossible acts would define us, because we walked with the power of the King of kings. A status quo Christian life wouldn't be tolerated by anyone who believed what the Bible says so firmly that he or she was determined to see its principles at work every day. Living a life defined by attaining all that God has scripted for us to bring Him glory would overtake our mental capacity and leave us speechless.

Does this kind of life sound impossible? Well, this can be a description of your life! So trash your way of thinking that you are a has-been. You have been appointed by God to be a main-stage player in God's plan. Get over your excuses, and fight for it!

To achieve significance, you must first of all *stop believing lies.*

Are you tired of feeling miserable? You may not outwardly manifest miserable emotions, but what about on the inside? When my ex-husband called me stupid for almost seven years, I chose to believe that I was stupid. You could not have told me otherwise. I had accepted a lie.

That lie almost tanked my life. I chose to accept as fact something that was a complete fallacy. I had decided to believe that repetitive phrase: "You are stupid." God certainly didn't tell me that from His Word. But I didn't check its reality with Scripture; therefore, I easily accepted it as the truth. Here's what Scripture tells us about Satan's character:

> You are of your father the devil, and you want to do the desires of your father. He was a murderer from the beginning, and does not stand in the truth because there is *no truth in him;* . . . he speaks from his own nature, for *he is a liar and the father of lies* (John 8:44, emphasis added).

This verse is paramount to understanding what you are up against. If Satan can get you to believe something that is false because you do not hold it under the accountability of Scripture, then he has won. Most of the time, the most harmful lies will be the ones that if not subjected to Scripture can steal what God has for you. If I walked around now and believed that I was stupid, I would never attempt the things God is asking me to do. Some days, I am still tempted to believe that lie, but I know that it is just that—a lie—and no longer will I accept it as truth.

Foundational Truth Is Where We Begin the Battle for Significance

Take a moment before reading further and identify any lies Satan has been telling you. All the lies from your past, the lies you believe right now and even the attack on your future need to be brought to light through the lens of what Scripture says. Today is the day to stop believing them. You need a clean slate. No form of spiritual legacy can result when built on a foundation of lies. It is time to substitute the lies for the truth that is only found in God's Word.

The Bible is the only barometer of truth, and it is true all the time and on all subjects, including you. God's perspective of you will differ from your perspective of yourself. You will most likely look at yourself and decide that you have too many problems to be used in a significant way by Him. The truth is that He made you intentionally for His purposes.

And you will know the truth, and the truth will make you free (John 8:32).

Begin to consistently shed biblical light on each lie you are tempted to believe and it will show you if you have believed a lie. After you understand that what you have believed is false, and Scripture sheds light on the issue, you are able to move forward in seeking your appointed role on earth.

Significance Is a Decision, Not a Natural Thought Pattern

You probably didn't look in the mirror this morning and say, "I am super-significant! I am awesome, and I lack nothing to achieve my calling." The thought that each of us is appointed for a specific purpose is not a natural thought pattern. Most times, we struggle even to accept compliments because we feel like we aren't good enough to receive them. To instinctively believe that we are amazing does not come naturally. I love it when people come to my house and compliment it, but my first response rather than saying thank you is to make an excuse why something isn't perfect. It is so hard for me just to accept that someone likes my house.

The decision to believe that you are appointed for a purpose, although it feels unnatural, is to accept the truth. God says that He created you for a purpose. Are you going to call God a liar? Umm, no. Changing your thought process will be challenging; but without that change, you will fail in seeking all that God has for you.

You are created for the glory of the Lord. Each act God asks of you is not ultimately for your benefit, but for His glory. When you understand that your calling and your achievement of all God has for you are actually for Him, it is much easier to accept the call.

You Have Everything Necessary

Genesis 1:31 tells us:

> God saw all that He had made, and behold, it was very good.

God made Adam and Eve with everything necessary to carry out their significant call. Nothing needed to be added to Adam or Eve to make them more qualified for their calling. They were created to do one of the most incredible jobs ever—to cultivate and farm the Garden of Eden.

Our minds trick us into believing that we must add to who we are to be people of significance. It's hard for us to accept that the eye color, hair color and personality traits we have are the exact ones that were planned for us. We look at ourselves and see blatant and raging problems. So does Satan. His outlook on you is to attack you where he knows it will hurt. He tempts you to believe that you lack something. But, sweet reader, God's outlook on you is that you are very good. Not one thing is missing that shouldn't be there. Not one thing was left out to cause you shame. Each unique trait was considered and executed by the powerful hand of the Master Craftsman. Your traits—from your weaknesses to your strengths—are very good.

With the team at The Blush Network, we celebrate strengths. There have been times when I've called one of my staff members just to tell them I appreciate how God made them. In times when I celebrate their strengths, I also celebrate my weaknesses. Because of my weaknesses, their strengths aid the ministry God has entrusted us with. Our team has a culture of celebrating each other (even the weird quirks in each of us) because we are created very good.

> Then the LORD God took the man and put him into the garden of Eden to cultivate it and keep it (Gen. 2:15).

Can you imagine knowing that God had just created the world and then He looked to you to make sure the Garden was properly maintained? What an amazing thing to be asked to do! Adam was also in charge of naming everything. What an honor! The names of every living thing we know of today are not the result of some nuclear scientist deciding on acceptable names; it was Adam's job. Adam didn't have a degree from Harvard or Yale. He wasn't a billionaire, nor had he written a best-selling novel. He didn't use a focus group to help with his calling from the Lord. He was simply presented with the task, and he obeyed.

The fact that Adam and Eve did their job is namely why we enjoy the lions and tigers at the zoo and can put the herbs basil and oregano in our spaghetti. They took their call seriously and didn't focus on the fact that they may not name the animals correctly or farm the land efficiently—they simply believed God. God had said that all He created was *very good*, and they chose to believe Him even when it came to them. In the very next verse, God told Adam and Eve the one rule they had to follow:

> The LORD God commanded the man, saying, "From any tree of the garden you may eat freely; but from the tree of the knowledge of good and evil you shall not eat, for in the day that you eat from it you will surely die" (Gen. 2:16-17).

Your Call Without an Evil Influence

If God's plan for your life wasn't affected by the enemy's evil influence, it might look easy. We look at Adam and Eve's purpose in the Garden and we think, *That wasn't that hard.* If I didn't have Satan attacking all the time, my job of leading The Blush Network would be much easier. When we choose to accept the challenge God gives us to follow through on a task that He has asked us to do, we seem to forget that if God has asked us to do it for His purpose, then Satan is against it.

Satan was lurking when God created Adam and Eve. He saw all the traits God poured into each of their souls. He saw the characteristics they were given as gifts to achieve the task God had set before them. He also was privy to the dictation of the one rule to not eat of the tree of the knowledge of good and evil. And he immediately started plotting evil.

Before that, Satan witnessed the creation of the universe. Read what God said to a man who challenged God's involvement in what was happening to him:

> Where were you when I laid the foundation of the earth?
> Tell Me, if you have understanding,
> Who set its measurements? Since you know.
> Or who stretched the line on it?
> On what were its bases sunk?
> Or who laid its cornerstone,
> When the morning stars sang together
> And all the sons of God shouted for joy? (Job 38:4-7).

God was talking to a man named Job in this passage; however, it indicates that the morning stars sang together and all the sons of God (angels) shouted for joy when the earth was created. The hosts of heaven literally praised God while He was creating the world and all that was in it. Satan was there because he was a cherub. After he was cast from heaven, Satan watched the attributes and characteristics of the male and female as God created them, and no doubt he took detailed notes.

Ezekiel 28:13 tells us:

> You were in Eden, the garden of God;
> Every precious stone was your covering:
> The ruby, the topaz and the diamond;
> The beryl, the onyx and the jasper;
> The lapis lazuli, the turquoise and the emerald;
> And the gold, the workmanship of your settings and
>   sockets,

Was in you.
On the day that you were created
They were prepared.

Satan was beautiful. He was the most beautiful thing God created. He was more beautiful than anything in the Garden of Eden, and all the trees were jealous of it:

The cedars in God's garden could not match it;
The cypresses could not compare with its boughs,
And the plane trees could not match its branches.
No tree in God's garden could compare with it in its
    beauty.
"I made it beautiful with the multitude of its branches,
And all the trees of Eden, which were in the garden of
    God, were jealous of it" (Ezek. 31:8-9).

Because of Satan's beauty, he has the appeal to sway you. His power is mostly limited to temptations and attempts to get you to give in to them. His goal is for you to give in to his appeal because he is ambitious about your forgoing your purpose, because it will bring God glory. He knows that if you push away from temptation and power through it, he has lost. So he'll try to get you to the point of hopelessness or distract you into choosing to live a life of ease because you think your life doesn't really matter.

Satan's Timing Is Strategic

Now the serpent was more crafty than any beast of the field which the LORD God had made. And he said to the woman, "Indeed, has God said, 'You shall not eat from any tree of the garden'?" The woman said to the serpent, "From the fruit of the trees of the garden we may eat; but from the fruit of the tree which is in the middle of the garden, God has said, 'You shall not eat from it or touch it, or you will die.'" The serpent said to the woman, "You surely will not die! For God knows that in the day you eat from it your eyes will be opened, and you will be like God, knowing good and evil" (Gen. 3:1-5).

Satan took great notes when Eve was created, and he strategically chose to approach her when she was alone. With one sentence, he questioned God's integrity and her intellect, which put her significance in danger. How many times does Satan come to us and ask a simple question such as, "Did God say that you really are important?" Maybe, "What was the rule on sex?" Even, "What did God say about having an abundant life?" Satan's timing is so strategic that the right question at the perfect time gets us to think, *Hmmm, did God really mean what He said?*

Don't Talk to Satan

Eve's biggest mistake was to engage in conversation with Satan to clarify what the exact rule was that God had given her. Her biggest problem was that she answered the question. If she had stopped Satan when she had the chance, he wouldn't have led her to the place of sin; however, she talked back, and the conversation heard around the world began.

We do the same thing. We mentally engage in conversation with Satan. When we engage in conversation with him, we give him power. Even the smallest response on our part invites his response. When Eve answered the question, Satan acted shocked that God would have told her she couldn't eat of the tree of the knowledge of good and evil. He said (paraphrased), "What? You will not surely die! You will be just like God and know exactly what He knows." This response got her thinking, *Do I want to be like God or just farm the garden?* The very thing Satan manipulated with Eve was her feeling of significance. God had already given Eve her call, which gave her great significance; if she had known the gravity of her call, she would have been honored.

Satan Strikes at Your Most Vulnerable Moments

Shortly after the Old Testament begins, it records sin entering the world; but watch how the New Testament begins with the answer to sin!

Before Jesus started His public ministry, Satan questioned and tempted Him while He was in the wilderness for a period of 40 days. In Matthew 4:1, the Bible says that Jesus was led by the Holy Spirit to be tempted by Satan. Jesus was in an incredibly vulnerable state. He hadn't eaten or drunk anything for 40 days, and when He was vulnerable, Satan made his move:

> After fasting forty days and forty nights, he was hungry. The tempter came to him and said, "If you are the Son of God, tell these stones to become bread." Jesus answered, "It is written: 'Man does not live on bread alone, but on every word that comes from the mouth of God.'" Then the devil took him to the holy city and had him stand on the highest point of the temple. "If you are the Son of God," he said, "throw yourself down. For it is written: 'He will command his angels concerning you, and they will lift you up in their hands so that you will not strike your foot against a stone.'" Jesus answered him, "It is also written: 'Do not put the Lord your God to the test.'" Again, the devil took him to a very high mountain and showed him all the kingdoms of the world and their splendor. "All this I will give you," he said, "if you will bow down and worship me." Jesus said to him, "Away from me, Satan! For it is written: 'Worship the Lord your God, and serve him only'" (Matt. 4:2-10, *NIV*).

Satan wanted to catch Jesus in a vulnerable state to try to sway His purpose on earth. Because Satan is the opposite of God, he uses moments of vulnerability and weakness to make us even weaker. His goal is to engineer our defeat. God's goal is to be our strength in our weakness.

Satan offered things to Jesus that weren't his to offer. He merely played on the circumstances of the moment. How can we assume that Satan would deal any differently with us? Notice that Jesus did not engage the great tempter in conversation—He shut him down with the Word of God. Satan departed only after Christ used Scripture. Because of that deliberate act on Jesus' part, His purpose on this earth was not affected, and Satan left. Satan's goal was to defeat Jesus before He even began His public ministry, but Jesus shut him down. Not so with Eve—she entered into a conversation with Satan rather than refusing to listen, and it led to her demise.

Positional Pride Is a Graveyard for Christians

Satan's first question to Jesus was to raise doubt about His position: "*If* you are the Son of God . . ." then prove it. Pride is a horrible stealer of significance. Being obsessed with a position you may hold now, and loving it too much, can rob you from taking a huge step of faith God wants you to take. If we hold our position too dearly, we will be tempted to defend that position even when God asks us to lay it down. Hold your position lightly. Your position in ministry or your job or your financial status will become an idol if you do not understand that the Lord only lends it to you.

Position is often mistaken as calling. Just because God has blessed you with position does not mean that at any time He cannot require it from you. Defending your small position is a sign of weakness. To achieve all that God has for you, be aware that it is not uncommon for Him to ask you to surrender the position you currently have to give you something greater. Jesus wasn't threatened by Satan's ploy, and therefore He wasn't defensive.

Manna Is No Match for God's Might

In Matthew 4:4, Jesus' reply to Satan when he asked Him to prove that He was the Son of God was, "Man shall not live by bread alone, but on every word that proceeds out of the mouth of God." Right answer!

There is probably no better example of man's utter need to depend on God's provision than in the story of the children of Israel during their long exodus from Egypt. We read the same words Jesus spoke to Satan in their story:

> He humbled you and let you be hungry, and fed you with manna which you did not know, nor did your fathers know, that He might make you understand that man does not live by bread alone, but man lives by everything that proceeds out of the mouth of the LORD (Deut. 8:3).

God allowed the Israelites to be hungry to drive them to dependence on Him. Manna is an immediate fix for a fleshly need. Our culture doesn't want for much. If we want something at the store, we borrow if we have to and buy it; immediate gratification steals from us the blessing of waiting on the Lord. We are even tempted to fix our sexual desires by having sex without being married or by looking at porn. When we fix our fleshly needs ourselves, we forfeit waiting on God and seeing how He can come in and do miracles for us. Depending on ourselves and not on God's power robs us of seeing what He could do for us.

There have been many needs in my home that I was tempted to not pray about and simply take care of through my own devices and control. Sometimes, I have failed in seeking God for my needs; but the times when I have prayed and sought God's power to meet my needs, He has blown me away. His answer was so much greater than anything I could have thought of. It's in those times that we build our dependence on the Lord, and our faith is strengthened. Seeing God's might paves the way for us to do whatever He asks us to do.

Satan's Use of Scripture vs. God's Use of Scripture

Then the devil took him to the holy city and had him stand on the highest point of the temple. "If you are the Son of God," he said, "throw yourself down. For it is written: 'He will command his angels concerning you, and they will lift you up in their hands so that you will not strike your foot against a stone.'" Jesus answered him, "It is also written: 'Do not put the Lord your God to the test'" (Matt. 4:5-7, *NIV*).

Notice in verse 6 that Satan began to use Scripture on Jesus. And then Jesus answered him with Scripture. Satan knows the Scriptures better than you do. He watched as the stories in Scripture played out in real time. He saw the prophets and giants from the pages of the Bible firsthand, as they lived. He will use Scripture as a weapon when it works in his favor. So you need to use wisdom in deciphering the difference between Satan's use of Scripture and the Lord's.

Satan's use of Scripture will completely throw you from what God is asking of you. It always speaks to a fleshly desire in you and normally evokes fear. His use always causes confusion and brings up questions on your part. For example: You are at a crossroads with a decision. God says to power through with faith. Satan will give you an excuse to wimp out. Never in the Bible does it say that it is okay to quit. It always says to be strong and press on.

God's use of Scripture is life giving. It always complements what the Holy Spirit is telling you. Even though God may be asking you to jump out in faith and do something that appears to be crazy, God's use of His Word always brings perfect peace. You will know when God speaks to you through His Word—when He does it is undeniable.

If Jesus had obeyed Satan's use of Scripture and "thrown Himself down," and His angels had come after Him, it would have disqualified Him from the cross, which was His ultimate calling.

When we interpret Scripture in a way that confuses God's obvious will throughout His Word, we are in danger of abandoning our calling.

Satan Offers What He Does Not Own

> Again, the devil took him to a very high mountain and showed him all the kingdoms of the world and their splendor. "All this I will give you," he said, "if you will bow down and worship me" (Matt. 4:8-9, *NIV*).

In an effort to lead you from where God wants you to go, Satan tends to offer you things that aren't his to offer. He may tell you things like, "Instead of taking that step of faith, stay right where you are; you will be happy here." He may lead you to believe that if you have sex only with your significant other before marriage, it's okay. He may tempt you to look at porn and tell you it will meet your sexual needs. Things that Satan cannot control he offers to us without any guarantee of getting them. He has no power to distribute peace and joy and fulfillment, but he is a professional at making you believe that he does. Stay alert; he will promise you something that may sound better in the moment than what God is asking of you. But it will be an empty promise.

A Bold Stance Causes Satan to Flee

> Jesus said to him, "Away from me, Satan! For it is written: 'Worship the Lord your God, and serve him only'" (Matt. 4:10, *NIV*).

Jesus took a bold stance and commanded Satan to leave. Because of the power that is in the name of Jesus, we have the opportunity to take that bold stance and tell Satan to be gone. Satan will leave when made to submit to God.

> Submit therefore to God. Resist the devil and he will flee from you (Jas. 4:7).

Satan's goal is to keep you from doing what you are placed on this earth to do. Remember, attacks of the enemy are a sure sign that you are working toward your significance. Stand and assume your position! Significance is yours for the taking. When you are resolute and decide to do exactly what God wants you to do to achieve His glory, you will be attacked, but none of those attacks will overcome you, because you have the power of God.

Satan will try to distract you, little by little, from attaining the true significance that is found in your calling in Christ. He will do it through money, stuff and even ministry. All these things he will use to masquerade as things that satisfy, even as he knows that God is the answer to finding your significance. He will whisper to you and say that you can be significant if . . . you look like her, or marry him, or have a ton of money. His purpose is to lead you further and further from the truth.

I wonder today if you have been lied to? Do you believe that you must be something you are not to make a difference? God says that all He made was *very good* (see Gen. 1:31). That includes you, my sweet friend. You need nothing added to you to make you more significant. You are significant just the way you were created.

Now your job is to explore the gifts and the call on your life to use it for Christ.

If you are a child of God, Scripture says that you are called with a holy calling (see 1 Tim. 1:9). You don't need to waste your life taking up space; you need to seek what that calling is and go for it unashamedly. In doing so, you will find the person God created you to be in an intimate relationship with Him. Challenge yourself today to be vigilant against the enemy's lies, and go after the truth.

I am so excited for your journey as you accept your calling and live as you were created to live! Seize your significance today!

QUESTIONS THAT SEEK TRUTH

1. Do you believe that you are significant? Based on the truth of your significance, how can your mark in the world make a difference?

2. I talk about the day when I lost the hope of ever being significant; have you experienced that? If so, describe what brought you to that conclusion?

3. With the realization that Satan is the father of lies (see John 8:44), what lies have you thought were true?

4. In order to believe that you are significant, you must start with truth. What does God's Word say that can help you counteract three major lies you have believed about yourself?

5. Because significance is not a natural thought pattern, write out an anthem for yourself that will remind you that you are perfectly placed on this earth for a purpose. What did you write as your first sentence?

6. According to Genesis 1:31, "God saw all that He had made, and behold, it was very good." Look at this verse as it applies to your strengths, your weaknesses and even your quirks. They are all at the exact level needed to achieve your calling. How do you see yourself now?

7. Satan was there when we were created, and he knows how to attack us. Given his advantage, what is one way that he continually attacks you?

8. Eve, in the Garden of Eden, engaged in conversation with Satan, which led to her demise. What conversation are you having with Satan that you need to shut down?
9. Sometimes we meet our physical needs without depending on the Lord. What do we stifle when we do that? Decide today to forego immediate gratification and depend on the Lord to supply your needs.
10. You have just read that Satan was there when the acts of Scripture were played out; he understands how to use Scripture to his advantage. What emotions does Satan's use of Scripture evoke versus God's use of Scripture?

2

The Significance of Insignificant Beginnings

Some days I simply exist, and it's very boring.
I constantly seek to discover my purpose, but I haven't found it yet.
I have an idea that I'm just waiting for it.

BLUSH ATTENDEE

Do you just exist, or does your purpose drive you?

The enemy works to discredit your origin. He is aware of both your physical and your spiritual births. He never gives up trying to make you accept the idea that either your physical birth or your spiritual birth is insignificant. When he succeeds in that persuasion, it creates exactly what he is aiming for, which is to cause you to put your potential into hibernation.

Hibernating one's potential in our Christian culture has led to the demise of it. The attack on our God-appointed capability has had and continues to have a colossal negative effect on living with significance.

If we Christians, as one unit, surrendered to our sovereign Lord and looked at ourselves as being the heirs of His powerful inheritance (see Eph. 1:11–14), we would hijack this culture and turn the tide. Such atrocities as abortion would be abolished; there would be no children in our foster care system, because they would be living in godly homes; the divorce rate would decrease to a startling low;

starving children would have access to food; pornography would be outlawed; our children wouldn't be having children; sexual abuse would be unheard of—all of these things would happen if we understood God enough to believe He has purposed us for something greater than we are living now.

What Causes Our Purpose to Go into Hibernation?

You may be someone who knows you have put your potential into a coma state. I am asking you today to consider God in your life's equation. If you put into hibernation what God wants you to become, you not only steal from your own achievements, but you also sacrifice your influence in our culture and suspend the opportunity for God to receive glory through you.

Reliance on the Flesh

One reason this happens is that as you grow physically and spiritually, you are vulnerable to attack. The enemy knows the amount of pressure to put on you to cause you to give up. Usually, it works. We need the power of God in us to overcome the relentless arrows the enemy hurls at us. When we try to fight back in our flesh, we lose.

God's words are clear about what we are to do:

Be strong in the Lord and in the strength of His might (Eph. 6:10).

It does not say, be strong in yourself and you'll figure it out. When fighting a ferocious spiritual battle, you cannot rely on yourself. That way leads to forfeiting the God-sized plan for which He has already drawn up the blueprint. Whatever God has appointed you to do, He will accomplish for you. Hibernating your potential is such a problem because it remains an option. You can choose to believe God's Word and stand boldly on the promises of God, or you can choose not to.

Submitting to Discouragement

Some of us get discouraged easily. Our calling is subject to human judgment. Most of us, when we are discouraged by human influence, give up or hibernate our potential. For example, when someone has the gift of song, she most likely begins singing alone in her bedroom, the car, the shower, and so on. When her confidence increases and she believes God wants to further her gift, she will begin singing for family. When family signs off on the talent, she will move on to singing for friends and eventually begin to make singing a calling.

Now, if any of these groups of people, including oneself, discourages the singing gift and begins to pick it apart, the person will be tempted to put her gift of song into hibernation, which will lead to a significant part of her life getting flushed down the toilet.

If you have the gift of song (which I do not have), the only acceptance you need is God's. If God has given you a gift, His full intention is for you to use it for His glory. However, be aware that you will face discouragement from human influence.

I cannot tell you how many times people have looked at me as if I had two heads while I was describing the calling God has on my life. I have been discouraged from achieving what God has for me, and at times the discouragement has been severe and heavy, simply because the enemy does not want my significance to be realized. I have had to stand on the Word of God for comfort when the attack is almost paralyzing.

The fight to achieve your potential will start at the beginning of both your physical and your spiritual births.

Belief in Satan's Lies

We all have a physical beginning: where we were born and raised; and we also can have a spiritual beginning: where we have surrendered to God and asked Him to be the Lord of our life. Satan attacks both our physical and our spiritual beginnings. He wants to disarm our potential, so he lies to us about our beginning. How does he do that? He may say things like, "You are nobody from nowhere" or "Nobody knows you; you are nothing."

When it comes to your spiritual beginning, he may say, "God has left you" or "Did you really mean what you said? You are such a sinner!" These thoughts can throw you off the path; but make no mistake, they have nothing to do with truth.

Physical Birth Is Recorded in Heaven

Both your physical beginning and your spiritual beginning are so significant that they are written in books in heaven! When you were born, your name was written in the book of life.

The goings-on in heaven paused as your name was entered. The beginning of life is of the utmost importance in heaven. Significance surrounded the moment you were brought into the world. The bells at the hospital were not the only thing that alerted the world of your existence; the pen of heaven was busy recording the magnificent event of your bith.

The book of life has every name of everyone who was ever born written in it, from Adam and Eve to the present:

> And I saw the dead, the great and the small, standing before the throne, and books were opened; and another book was opened, which is the book of life; and the dead were judged from the things which were written in the books, according to their deeds (Rev. 20:12).

Psalm 139:16 also speaks of the book of life when David says:

> Your eyes have seen my unformed substance; and in Your book were all written the days that were ordained for me, when as yet there was not one of them.

Moses spoke about it when he stood before God and asked forgiveness for the Israelites' sin of idolatry. If their sin was too great, Moses said, then as their leader his name should be blotted out from the book of life: "But now, if You will, forgive their sin—and if not, please blot me out from Your book which you have written" (Exod. 32:32). (Read the whole story and see how God responded to Moses' request.)

Satan would have you believe otherwise about your beginning, but that is in direct opposition to Scripture. You see, sweet reader, you are included in a book that God is the author of. He wrote your name in it because He planned great things for you.

Many strategic attacks have been placed on the unborn, none so deadly as abortion. The stolen significance of an unborn creation of God has Satan winning before the battle is even allowed to begin.

In Scripture, we see that Moses was almost a victim of infant murder when Pharaoh murdered all the Hebrew babies. We see the same technique used by Herod when he found out Jesus had been born; all little boys two years of age and younger were sentenced to death in Herod's attempt to wipe out the prophesied Messiah.

Satan instigated the idea of abortion long before Roe vs. Wade. It is a modern-day "fix" to what the culture demands, but it is an age-old problem. The problem in Moses' and Jesus' days was that both of the leaders of those worlds were making a decision to rid the world of male children who would produce potential. Killing them at a young age would solve the problem, they thought, of making sure their kingdoms were protected.

In our modern-medicine age, abortion kills babies before they even take their first breath. Satan may have convinced our culture that abortion serves the purpose of convenience, but make no mistake, the lives of significant and, no doubt, spiritual giants have been slain as our world feeds on this poison.

Spiritual Birth Is Recorded in the Lamb's Book of Life

Then there is the Lamb's book of life. Everyone who makes the decision to become a child of God has their name written in this book. When you decided to become a follower of Jesus, your name was recorded in the Lamb's book of life. I love that the name is the "Lamb's book of life." When you read of the animal sacrifices in Scripture, you see that a perfect lamb was required as a willing, submissive animal that would be sacrificed for the sin of the people.

Jesus became that perfect Lamb for us, and He offered the ultimate sacrifice for our sin. The name "Lamb's book of life" is a reminder of the spotless Lamb slain before the foundation of the world and then literally slain in time, on a cross, in order to give us eternal life.

> Nothing unclean, and no one who practices abomination and lying, shall ever come into it, but only those whose names are written in the Lamb's book of life (Rev. 21:27).

Satan wants to prevent your spiritual beginning. If he cannot stop your physical beginning, he will try to steal your spiritual birth.

He does not want you to be added to God's army. He plots from the moment you are born to try to keep you from your spiritual beginning. When he cannot stop your spiritual beginning, he tries to make you believe that it was insignificant.

It may look small from a human standpoint, but God's Word says this about it: "I tell you that in the same way, there will be more joy in heaven over one sinner who repents than over ninety-nine righteous persons who need no repentance" (Luke 15:7). Both your physical beginning and your spiritual beginning are so celebrated in heaven! Why do we here on earth think we are of no significance? Answer: *to keep us from seeing truth.*

The reason we love movies where the small-town sports team wins a national championship is because their greatest potential has been realized. We root for the underdog as they prepare to annihilate the champion team.

You may feel like that small-town athlete today, but I want you to know that God's desire for your life, whatever that may be, will have the same ending as "small-town team annihilates the big guy" if God is your focus. First, your expectation for your life must die. Human expectation is laughable compared to God's capability. You do not know what is best for you. You can't know, because you have no idea what the future holds. God's perspective of your life is in its entirety. He pieced your life together before time began, and it is a piece in His eternal plan for the world. Do you see that? Your life in this age is an intricate part of a much larger plan.

No architect would build a beautiful building as he goes along. The architect works for months and sometimes years ahead of time before the foundation of the completed building is even laid. Meticulous thought is put into each step, and the material is pristinely crafted for the finished building. God, as the first architect, knows where you fit in His completed product. The only way to achieve maximum use and effectiveness and blessing is by choosing Him as the focus of your life. What you think is best for your life, God may not agree with. This trips people up all the time.

When your name entered the Lamb's book of life, you chose to make God the Savior of your life. At that time, all things became new, including the power of the Holy Spirit in your life. The Holy Spirit's role is to lead, guide and direct. Trust me, the Holy Spirit will speak to you. Listening to what the Holy Spirit speaks to your spirit is how you can achieve what God purposes for your life.

Most of the time, becoming what God wants is as simple as listening. One devotional book put it as simple as "Mind the checks." When we are headed the wrong way, the Holy Spirit will speak to our spirit with angst and almost scream at us with unrest in our spirit. On the other hand, if we are headed down the right path, although it may look crazy, the Holy Spirit will give us a peace that people are in awe of. Peace and rest in your spirit are sure signs that you are headed in the right direction. Angst is a sure sign that you need to turn around.

My husband and I bought a boat many years ago. We loved this boat, but a couple of years ago we were getting ready to move. Eddie wanted to sell the boat so that we didn't have to move with it. We listed the boat on the Internet. Well, we got a call one day from a guy who was really interested. We went to meet him and he seemed nice enough, but in my spirit something was screaming at me. I felt very uncomfortable about this particular man, and for some reason, I didn't want him to buy the boat. However, Eddie moved forward and sold it to this particular guy. Long story short, and a year later, we still hadn't received full payment for the boat and didn't have possession of the boat. The Holy Spirit had literally told me to listen, but we didn't.

The same guidance will work in your specific callings. God will change your expectations of your life and factor Himself in when you become His child.

My Small Beginnings

I grew up in Terre Haute, Indiana, where the population was approximately 60,000 people. My childhood home was the picture of comfort. The yard welcomed you like a welcome mat with large overgrown trees that towered over the split-level house. Those trees became a sanctuary for many games, laughter and the occasional injury. When you walked into my childhood home, you would often be greeted with the aroma of freshly baked bread or roast beef slowly cooking in the oven. (As I think of it today, my mouth waters from the memory of how those meals tasted.)

The galley kitchen was the scene of frequent laughter as my dad teased us about the events of the day. My mercy-showing mother would be our protection when his infectious, boisterous personality took over. My sister, brother and I have vivid memories of things like the underwear monster attacking us (our dad with underwear on his head), or the man with the drippy fingers (my mom's legendary story of a man whose fingers dripped through the vents in our house), or "get Daddy down" night (when we all attacked my dad and wrestled him until he got tired).

The covered bridge festival (huge fall flea market), Carey Cry fest (which happens every Thanksgiving and is us telling each other how much we appreciate each other), and regular trips to the state park, Turkey Run, are cemented in my mind as pillars of joy from my youth.

Even though my childhood was pleasant, the battle for my significance raged. My peaceful childhood home didn't protect me from believing the lies that were hurled at me.

Growing up, I remember envisioning myself as being the CEO of a company. I can remember closing my eyes and watching myself walk out of a high-rise office building and get into a cab in downtown New York City. Back then, that's all I knew; I wanted to be the CEO of a company. But even though I wanted to be a CEO, I believed it was impossible. I placed my own potential in hibernation for a time due to my circumstances. Satan had me believing that my beginning was so insignificant that the thought of even attempting my dream would be laughable.

Don't get me wrong; in my childhood years, I believed I did have some potential. But as I grew older and listened to words of discouragement such as, "You are an airhead" or "You will never get out of this small town," my potential slowly slipped into hibernation, and I waved my white flag of surrender, standing on a foundation of lies. Believing that I would be fighting a losing battle made me shut down my dream. Believing that my beginning was insignificant and my existence was without effect, I became the victim of my own story.

Later in life, I met Jesus. Now I have no desire to be the CEO of a company in New York; however, I do have a passion for reaching our world for Christ, and in doing so, God allowed me to be the founder and president of The Blush Network, which is an organization that reaches young women with truth. When God became my focus, He changed my dream to what He wanted for my life.

Bring Your Significance Out of Hibernation

Perhaps today you are sitting with your potential in hibernation. There is a way out; you must stand up and begin to cut through the lies as if you were using a machete to cut through a thick rain forest. Your beginning, though it may have been small to human eyes, was great in heaven.

Take a closer look at your physical beginning: your birthday. Satan will try to belittle the circumstances if you were perhaps born in a small town, the inner city or a different country. I see such an attack on single-parent homes and families that are poor. Know this: Your circumstances do not define you.

I believe that we are living in a day and age when we become both the victim and the villain of our own lives. A victim will blame all that has happened to her on circumstances. This is a sure sign of potential in hibernation. The victim individual feels entitled to feelings of insignificance because her circumstances don't say otherwise. Our culture has gotten so tied up in feeding feelings that many of us let our feelings control our actions. We think that if we feel insignificant, it means we are, and that attitude steals potential.

Don't Be Your Own Villain

If you believe that you are of no importance because of humble beginnings, you may have become the villain in your own life. You may have turned to an addiction such as pornography, alcohol, self-mutilation, drugs or sex. You may have drowned your soul with what you think will take the pain away—the pain of the circumstances of your childhood that make you feel like no one will ever care about you. You may have accepted a belief that you will never amount to anything, and you are determined to do what you want with your life. You have rebelliously proclaimed in your heart that you are your own god.

If so, your life is in danger of being wasted on being controlled by fleeting emotions and damaging actions—a victory for evil.

The right approach is to choose to champion your circumstances and become the victor of them.

I want to challenge your thinking. Could it be that God placed you in the very home you were raised in, with any number of dire circumstances, in order to prepare you for an effective calling? Could it be that the challenges you have faced are the education you will need to persevere in your avenue of service?

Be a Victor Instead

Let's look at the example of Jesus' life. The Holy Spirit was the One who conceived Jesus in Mary. She was poor and very young, and her family was not recognized in the city. She had no form of influence in the town. She was simply a small-town girl engaged to marry a man named Joseph. God looked beyond what appeared to be an insignificant girl and saw an obedient spirit. God was impressed with Mary's internal wow factor and chose her to carry His Son.

As the story goes in the Gospels, the angel Gabriel appeared to Mary with the greeting, "Favored one." Gabriel didn't look at her and say, "Hey there, wealthy one" or "What's up, famous girl?" God didn't care about the circumstances of Mary's life. He was most interested in her heart. Mary could have complained about the poor life she was living, but she didn't, and God blessed her by choosing her to be the mother of His Son.

Fast-forward nine months when Mary goes into labor with the Christ child. As we know from the recorded story in the Gospels, Jesus was born in a stable in the city of Bethlehem (see Luke 2:7). The world was almost completely oblivious to the birth of the Messiah, and didn't care, except for the shepherds who were alerted by the Angel of the Lord and the wise men who saw the star and followed its path to Bethlehem.

On that Christmas night, I can imagine the name of Jesus Christ being written so strategically in the book of life, and the throne room of heaven erupting with excitement as Mary brought forth the Christ Child. However, there was not much of a sound on the earth. What seemed like an afterthought on earth was a complex plan conceived before the foundation of the world to save the world!

Jesus' story is a story of victory. He wasn't confined to the insignificance of His birth; He was trained by it. He wasn't discouraged that He wasn't born into wealth on earth; His heavenly Father was rich. Jesus' beginning was small and seemingly insignificant, but His end changed the world.

Sweet reader, you need to change your way of thinking. Choose to be the victor in your story.

My Spiritual Battles

There has never been a day that compares to the day I met Jesus. That day my mind changed forever. For the first time, I felt the meaning of joy. My euphoria after being blind to spiritual things for so long, and finally having the blinders peeled away, gave me hope. I became passionate about Jesus, and that passion still lives in me today. I am a firm believer that once you have experienced God's power of forgiveness in your life, you can never be the same as you were.

I began my love affair with Jesus in a very small way. There was no crowd, no pomp and circumstance, just a surrendered heart and God as the audience of one. I believed for the first time that God had a plan for me, and like the words that described the apostle Paul's spiritual beginning, God had a specific plan for me.

> But the Lord said to him, "Go, for he is a chosen instrument of Mine, to bear My name before the Gentiles and kings and the sons of Israel" (Acts 9:15).

I finally believed that God wanted to use all I had to glorify His Name.

Wounded by Satan's Attacks

Satan saw the transformation too. He watched as I yielded to the urging of the Holy Spirit, and he was ready to do all he could to immobilize my future. It worked. When I sinned, Satan wouldn't let me forget it. Guilt would paralyze me as I tried to seek forgiveness and move on.

Lies, sex and self-obsession began to consume me as I continued to give Satan a foothold in my life. Overcome with the burden of disappointing the almighty God, I completely gave myself over to my flesh. I may have been a child of God, but you wouldn't know it. My spiritual significance was in hibernation. Satan had me just where he wanted me. He couldn't take my salvation from me, but he could tempt me to become ineffective for spiritual use. By the time my sin was done with me, I was lying facedown at 3:00 A.M. in a mess of circumstances.

When Christians hibernate, Satan's hordes cheer. You don't have to be addicted to drugs or porn to be in hibernation; the enemy only needs you to be lazy. The lazy Christian does more harm to our culture than the rebellious non-Christian. The lasting impact is much more severe.

Christian, have you swallowed the lie that your role as a Christian is not that important? Do you go to church and then leave it behind? Do you ever share the name of Jesus with someone who needs to hear it? Do you read your Bible? Do you understand that the power of God is waiting for you to utilize it?

I fear that we will be shocked when we get to heaven by the number of people who are not present. Why is it in our churches that 10 percent of the people are doing 100 percent of the work? Why is it that our churches are struggling so much financially in the richest country in the world? Because we have let ourselves go. Spiritually, we are weak and out of shape. Awake, Church! Awake! Seize back the years the locusts have eaten! Seize them back! They are yours for the taking!

My Birth Right Reclaimed

Facedown, at 3:00 A.M., my significance came out of hibernation. I feebly flexed my spiritual muscles and offered a weak prayer. When I opened my Bible, the words on the page spoke so powerfully to me that it changed my life. I had to make a decision that night that I would not live an ineffective life for the Lord. I consciously decided amidst all the circumstances I found myself in that I was going to follow the Lord and accept all that He had for me.

My fear that night was that God was risky; what if God didn't accept me? I had broken all my promises to Him to keep His way, and I was worried that He was mad; but He was waiting for me with His arms open wide, saying, *I'm here, Autumn. I forgive you.*

When helpless humans put their hands into the hand of what they think is a risky God, they find ultimate stability instead. There was no one in the room that night as I chose to recommit my life to the Lord. It seemed insignificant, but it serves today as the turning point for my life. Sometimes, we have to begin again. That is the beauty of the cross and forgiveness.

> For this is contained in Scripture, "Behold, I lay in Zion a choice stone, a precious corner stone, and he who believes in Him will not be disappointed" (1 Pet. 2:6).

Once I had decided to completely surrender again to the Lord, I had to slam my life down upon the Chief Cornerstone. I needed a rock to stabilize the destruction I had caused in my life, and little by little, I started to rebuild. The more I built, the more aware I was of the attacks of the enemy trying to steal my spiritual significance.

Small Beginning, but Big Ending

I get excited when I think of what God can do with you. If this generation dares to fight back what evil has stolen, we are promised victory! Victory is promised to us through the power of God—but the Bible never says it will not take a fight.

> Therefore everyone who hears these words of Mine and acts on them, may be compared to a wise man who built his house on the rock. And the rain fell, and the floods came, and the winds blew and slammed against that house; and yet it did not fall, for it had been founded on the rock (Matt. 7:24-25).

When you resurrect your decision to make God the Lord of your life, even though you may have to fight through rough storms in order to achieve your purpose, you will not fall.

> The steps of a man are established by the LORD, and He delights in his way. When he falls, he will not be hurled headlong, because the LORD is the One who holds his hand (Ps. 37:23-24).

When you are born, you are a person of potential and promise, no matter what your actual circumstances might be. Do not go through life without having realized your potential and promise. Live your life by seizing and exercising the power of the Most High to achieve those things planned for you. I fear that too many people die without realizing what they were made to do. Be resolute about leaving a legacy for the generations after you. Do not let your end mirror your beginning. End your life satisfied that you exhausted all avenues of service to the King.

The end of Jesus' parable about the house on the rock versus the house on the sand goes like this:

> Everyone who hears these words of Mine and does not act on them, will be like a foolish man who built his house on the sand. The rain fell, and the floods came, and the winds blew and slammed against that house; and it fell—and great was its fall (Matt. 7:26-27).

Scripture tells us that Satan's fall will be great. In chapter 1, we talked about the beginning of Satan. Satan's beginning was amazing. He was the most beautiful creature ever created. But what will be his end?

> Then I saw an angel coming down from heaven, holding the key of the abyss and a great chain in his hand. And he laid hold of the dragon, the serpent of old, who is the devil and Satan, and bound him for a thousand years; and he threw him into the abyss, and shut it and sealed it over him, so that he would not deceive the nations any longer, until the thousand years were completed; after these things he must be released for a short time. . . . And the devil who deceived them was thrown into the lake of fire and brimstone, where the beast and the false prophet are also; and they will be tormented day and night forever and ever (Rev. 20:1-3,10).

Whew, that's heavy. Satan's beginning was beautiful and full of purpose to bring God glory; but he chose not to follow God's design for him, and his end is doom. His end will be the antithesis of his beginning.

Compare Satan's beginning to Jesus' beginning, which was small in the eyes of the world. Jesus' end on earth was magnificently glorious. Jesus reached His maximum potential, while Satan squandered his. Jesus' beginning may have been small from an earthly standpoint, but great is His end.

> And he who sits on the throne said, "Behold, I am making all things new." And He said, "Write, for these words are faithful and true." Then He said to me, "It is done. I am the Alpha and the Omega, the beginning and the end. I will give to the one who thirsts from the spring of the water of life without cost" (Rev. 21:5-6).

I desperately desire my life to reach its maximum potential. Isn't that what you desire too? As you sit reading this, know that your end will blow your mind if you are yielded to our great God. Start today and decide from this point forward to choose to be transformed into exactly what God wants for you. I adore you.

> Though your beginning was insignificant, yet your end will increase greatly (Job 8:7).

QUESTIONS THAT SEEK TRUTH

1. The enemy wants to discredit your origin. Note a time, if any, when you downplayed the origin of your birth or your hometown. What was the occasion?
2. Is your potential in hibernation? How do you know that?
3. Knowing that your physical beginning was entered into the book of heaven the moment you were born, how does that knowledge affect your feeling of inadequacy?
4. Satan wants to stop your name from being written in the Lamb's book of life because he knows you can achieve huge things for the Lord. Describe an attack placed on you by the enemy when you made the decision to become a Christian. How did you overcome it?

5. The moment you open your heart and your life to God, you immediately have a spiritual calling and gifts to execute it. What has God been laying on your heart that you know you need to use your gifts to execute?

6. Being a victim of your circumstances steals your focus on your purpose. What are some areas in your life that you have blamed on your upbringing?

7. Have you been the villain of your own story? That is, have you been your own worst enemy? Explain.

8. I want you to bring your significance out of hibernation. What three actions are you going to complete in order to do so?

9. Satan's beginning was huge, but his end is doom. How can you do just the opposite and have your ending be bigger than your beginning?

10. Jesus' beginning was small, but He was a victor all the way to the end. Since we have been given such a great example in His victorious life, spend some time in prayer, asking God for strength to do the same. What do you feel strengthened to do as a result of your prayer time?

Thoughts

* A Place Called Grace

* Something w/ Terri

* Talk to the gal @ group tonight.

3

The Significance of Intimacy with Christ

I wish I felt significant.

BLUSH ATTENDEE

What role does intimacy with Christ play in your life?

I let Satan take control of my mind and swallowed his lie that God hated me. As I lay in frozen silence beside the man I had married just two years earlier, my heart was pumping so rapidly that I could almost imagine a machine gun shooting me through the heart.

I stared up at the ceiling and watched the flutter of light from the TV still going in the early hours of the morning. So many thoughts were running through my mind. *God wants you dead,* taunted me, followed by, *You have committed the worst sin possible,* and *No one will ever love you.*

God hates you was a thought I almost couldn't bear, but I believed it, and I lay there completely terrified of God. I would go to sleep in the wee hours of the morning and wake only a few hours later, grateful each time I awoke, because I "knew" that God wanted to kill me in my sleep. I had swallowed the lie that God hated me. As far as I could tell, God had turned His back on me and would no longer extend any more grace to me. He was done with me.

When I drove my car, I would shake. I believed that if God let me wake in the morning, He would surely make me get into a fatal car accident. So I would only drive a few miles from my house. If I had to drive any farther, I was filled with fear until I reached my destination. I couldn't watch any scary movie or watch any hour-long police drama, because I knew that one day I would be the star in my own tragic drama.

I attended a small Baptist church my dad pastored in my home-town in Indiana. I remember trying to keep my mind busy during almost every sermon because I didn't think the truth applied to me. I would do anything to skip the worship, because I was terrified of entering God's glorious presence knowing exactly how He felt about me. Thoughts of suicide would come and go.

However, I was terrified that God wanted to kill me, so I was at a crossroads on the subject of death. I was in a psychological prison—a captive to my own thoughts.

Just nine years earlier, in 1992, I had asked Jesus to be my Savior on a beautiful Easter Sunday after church. I remember sitting on the side of the bathtub in our pale yellow bathroom, with tears streaming down my flushed cheeks, pondering the words that were clearly presented in church just hours earlier. After years of hearing about Jesus and knowing that He was God's Son sent to die on the cross for my sin, the story resonated within me. I realized that I was someone whom Jesus died for. *Me!* The story was not for someone else. I desperately needed the blood He shed to take away sin.

I had felt separated from God my whole life, and it seemed like that day I realized what that separation was. It was my sin, and all I knew was that I couldn't bear it any longer. I wanted that separation gone. I thought, *If God is as good as everyone says He is, I want to know Him more.*

My dad walked by and paused as he noticed his happy-go-lucky girl sobbing. He asked me what was wrong, and I explained that I wanted Jesus to be my Savior. My dad asked me some clarifying questions about what had brought me to that decision, and con-vinced of my intense desire, he led me in prayer.

I remember praying as earnestly as I could, asking God to for-give me of my sins. I finally believed that He died for me. It wasn't just a feel-good story to listen to on Easter; it was truth. I knew that day that I needed to be wiped clean from my sin. My heart couldn't contain the joy after we said "Amen." I was made brand new.

"Prone to Wander, Lord, I Feel It . . ."

I hadn't thought of that day in years. As I lay frozen with fear at three in the morning, only the creaks from the settling of the house accompanied my thoughts. What happened? Where did I lose that assurance of God's sacrificial love for me? How did I go from once being passionate about His love for me and telling anyone who would listen at my school to believing that He hated me so badly that He wanted me dead?

Something told me to get up and go into the office, which was directly across from our bedroom. I slowly and cautiously got up out of bed and tiptoed into the other room, quietly closing the door behind me so that I wouldn't wake my husband. I flipped the light switch and squinted, questioning what I was doing. I sank into the hand-me-down dingy blue couch that had been severely broken in over the years. My arm rested on a piece of tar that had been embedded in the fabric years earlier. I began to pick at this piece of tar with my fingernail. *Click, click, click* was the only noise in the quiet house for many minutes.

I didn't know how to approach God. I hadn't picked up my Bible in a year. Every time I saw it, I trembled, believing that it would only tell me of all my sin and confirm that God was judging my every move. Oh, I knew that I had screwed up. I knew that I was a sinner. I knew that every premarital sexual experience and lie that I had told to cover it up made me one of the worst of sinners. I knew that I should never have married the man I did, but I did it because that's what I wanted. I knew that every time I went out and partied on Saturday and then went to church on Sunday with a heart far from God was a slap in God's face. On Sundays, I paraded like a saint, all the while living a double life. Saint on Sunday, sinner on Monday became routine, and I grew numb to the things of God.

That night, however, even while in a state of torture, it was like something was calling me in my soul. Enough was enough. I had come to a crossroads. Because of my choices, I was living in a prison and I couldn't bear it any longer. Something had to give. I needed help!

As I sat on that blue couch, I had two choices: to end my life or try God again. I didn't want to kill myself, so that left me with one option: God. I glanced across the room and my eye caught my blue Bible. I stared at it for what seemed like an hour. Finally, I mustered up enough courage to touch it with a trembling hand and sweaty palm. I grabbed the Bible. I looked up to heaven and gave God a challenge. It went something like this: *If You are truly the God that You say You are, I need You now. If You are so good, I need Your goodness. If You are all powerful, then speak to me now. I am desperate.*

My Chains Fell Off

With that, I closed my eyes and flipped the Bible open. My blood-shot eyes rested on one verse: "Long life is the reward of the righteous" (Prov. 16:31, *GNB*). I dropped the Bible. Then, in a state of shock, I read the verse again: "Long life is the reward of the righteous." I dropped to my knees as the intensity of the might of God seemed to fill the room.

This verse spoke to my very soul. God addressed the biggest fear in my life with one sentenwce. The thought of inevitable and impending death had plagued me for one solid year, and in one sentence the Word of God dispelled my deep darkness like a beam of light shining into a dark dungeon. In that moment, my bondage turned to hope. In that unexplainable moment, power prevailed. The grip of lies loosened and I was set free.

I lay prostrate before the Lord for some time. I cried out to Him for forgiveness and received renewed strength to battle my circumstances. I was in awe of God meeting me in the very height and depth of my sin, reaching His hand down to where I was and pulling me toward Him. I didn't need to be clean. I didn't need to be perfect. I just needed to dare to believe that He was God and that He could save me from my distress.

My Heart Was Free

It was that night that I surrendered fully to the Lord. I'm not sure how long I prayed that night, but when I stood up, I was a resurrected soul who had just experienced the true Spirit of the Most High God. Since that night, I have never been the same. I went back to bed and slept like I hadn't slept in years. Peace had entered my soul, and I was changed because of it.

And on His robe and on His thigh He has a name written, "KING OF KINGS, AND LORD OF LORDS" (Rev. 19:16).

In the days that followed my surrender, I found myself waiting for my husband to leave the house; when I heard the garage door close, I would run into the office and spend time with my God. I was so hungry, so desperate for Him. My life took on a whole new outlook. Now my life seemed to be one of promise, of hope. I would turn on worship music and weep over my Bible and pray, only to look at the clock and see that two hours had passed. Not wanting to leave, I would remain until the duties of life called. I was desperate for more of God.

Although the circumstances of my life hadn't changed, I had, because the King of kings and the Lord of lords had touched me, and I was *never going back!*

Don't you want to know the King of kings and Lord of lords? God's greatest reality for your life is impossible to attain unless you have an intimate relationship with Him.

Let's Get Real

Picture a relationship that meets your every desire for acceptance, comfort and love. Imagine what it would be like to never be hurt or disappointed in this relationship. You would never be betrayed, abused or mistreated. What if on your darkest, loneliest day, there was someone who spoke the most personal truth to your soul to encourage you to go on. What if every mistake you had ever made was changed into victory because of this relationship.

Imagine that trust was never an issue. You never had to hold back or pretend to be someone else. You never had to impress; you just had to be. Your wildest dreams came true at your request, just because you are loved. You got to have conversations that are authentic and honest, and you never wondered if you were judged or gossiped about. You knew you would be understood.

What if you stood alone, but you always had support? And every time you met with this person, you felt refreshed. And what if no matter what happened in your life, you could be assured that it would work out as good?

Of course, we would all say, "I want that! That's what I need right now! How do I get that?" Let me show you from God's Word what it takes. We learn from our example, Jesus:

> Then Jesus went with his disciples to a place called Gethsemane, and he said to them, "Sit here while I go over there and pray." He took Peter and the two sons of Zebedee along with him, and he began to be sorrowful and troubled. Then he said to them, "My soul is overwhelmed with sorrow to the point of death. Stay here and keep watch with me." Going a little farther, he fell with his face to the ground and prayed, "My Father, if it is possible, may this cup be taken from me. Yet not as I will, but as you will." Then he returned to his disciples and found them sleeping. "Couldn't you men keep watch with me for one hour?" he asked Peter. "Watch and pray so that you will not fall into temptation. The spirit is willing, but the flesh is weak." He went away a second time and prayed, "My Father, if it is not possible for this cup to be taken away unless I drink it, may your will be done." When he came back, he again found them sleeping, because their eyes were heavy. So he left them and went away once more and prayed the third time, saying the same thing. Then he returned to the disciples and said to them, "Are you still sleeping and resting? Look, the hour is near, and the Son of Man is betrayed into the hands of sinners. Rise! Let us go! Here comes my betrayer!" (Matt. 26:36-46, *NIV*).

I shudder at the example of Jesus in the garden. We worship Him as our Savior and the Son of the living God. He was also fully man. Imagine the absolute trepidation that plagued the God man as He waited in the garden for His destiny to be fulfilled. The power of death taunted Him as He articulated His feelings to His disciples:

> Then he said to them, "My soul is overwhelmed with sorrow to the point of death. Stay here and keep watch with me" (v. 38).

He knew the terror that was His destiny; He was at the brink of fully being reconciled with His purpose and was vulnerable enough to His disciples to let them hear His distress. The Creator articulating need to the Creation screams His vulnerable state.

Then He changes His focus to communicate with His Father:

> Going a little farther, he fell with his face to the ground and prayed, "My Father, if it is possible, may this cup be taken from me. Yet not as I will, but as you will" (v. 39).

The sheer deposit of stress weighing down His mind forced the most vulnerable position of prayer. We see a man begging God for another option, yet understanding the need for His obedience. After checking in with His disciples, and asking them to please pray after finding them asleep, He returns to the intimacy that is not found in the relationship with the disciples, but with God alone.

> He went away a second time and prayed, "My Father, if it is not possible for this cup to be taken away unless I drink it, may your will be done" (v. 42).

A second time He begs, and a second time He acknowledges that no matter what, He was not interested in His own will, but in the will of the Father.

He came back to the disciples in verse 43 and found them sleeping again. When He saw this, after asking His friends' support in prayer, He returned to seek God's face a third time.

I couldn't talk about intimacy with Christ without giving the example of the relationship Jesus Himself had with God the Father. Jesus knew exactly what His purpose was. We also see this represented in Luke 2:49, when He tells Joseph and Mary, who were seeking their 12-year-old son, that He was about His Father's business.

Being fully man, Jesus was faced with the option of being obedient to the cross. God the Father selected God the Son to become incarnated to walk through the most horrifying trial known to humankind. His very purpose was to suffer and die while taking the entire sin of the world on Himself (see 1 Pet. 2:24). His purpose was to experience brutality as payment for sins He did not commit;

it was for you and me so that we could be counted as righteous to a holy God.

Being fully man, there is no way that Jesus would have finished His sacrificial purpose without the intense intimacy He had with God the Father. He knew God's purpose for Him. His relationship with God the Father was the only thing at that point in the garden that He could count on; it was the only thing that was keeping Him on track. It wasn't the disciples; and at that point it wasn't the cross; it was the fact that He could trust in His Father. He understood that all earthly desires in that garden paled in comparison to His relationship with God, which made the cross bearable. Jesus would rather have endured the cross with God the Father than choose not to do it without Him.

He endured it all for the will of the Father; and on the third day after His burial, He rose again, having paid for our sins and having conquered death.

We now have access to Jesus as our mediator between God and man. The access that Jesus provided for us on the cross makes it possible to have an intimate relationship with Father God (see 1 Tim. 2:5-6). Divine confidence and support are yours when the world is completely weighing you down to the point of desperation. But it's a choice. You can decide to forgo your right to participate in the most unbelievable relationship you have ever dreamed of, or you can choose to figure out life with your "disciples" who will inevitably fall asleep on you at some point.

To me, there is no comparison. I have tasted and seen, and I am convinced that no human will ever stand in for my relationship with God. My purpose demands strength that is only available through knowing that my God is for me.

Have You Made the Choice?

> Behold, I stand at the door and knock. If anyone hears my voice and opens the door, I will come in to him and eat with him, and he with me (Rev. 3:20, *ESV*).

To begin or to cultivate intimacy with Christ, you must first take a look at where you are spiritually.

Review

Intimacy with Christ begins on the foundation of truth. Take a minute to review your spiritual life. When was the last time you prayed? When was the last time you read your Bible aside from being at church? When was the last time you heard God's voice spoken clearly to you? Be honest; on a scale of 1 to 10, where would you rank your relationship with God? Do you even have a relationship with Him? Beginning today, acknowledging the truth of your spiritual state is your starting point. Once you have determined this, you can build on it, like a house.

> Everyone then who hears these words of mine and does them will be like a wise man who built his house on the rock. And the rain fell, and the floods came, and the winds blew and beat on that house, but it did not fall, because it had been founded on the rock. And everyone who hears these words of mine and does not do them will be like a foolish man who built his house on the sand. And the rain fell, and the floods came, and the winds blew and beat against that house, and it fell, and great was the fall of it (Matt. 7:24-27, *ESV*).

I hear women say all the time, "I don't have time to read the Bible." I call, *bull!* Truth is, you probably had time to watch that reality TV show last night and update your Facebook status. Time is an issue of choice. You choose where to spend your time. People say, "I'm busy," but they are choosing the busy life they lead. I get it, there are things we must do, such as work and duties at home. However, you cannot be successful in those must-do things unless you have an intimate relationship with your Creator. Without starting and cultivating an intimate relationship with Christ, your must-do things will never be as successful as if they were discussed with God and God gave you clear direction on them.

My sweet reader, other things must wait. I guarantee that if you begin to choose to spend time with God, you will begin to benefit. Now hear me, that does not exclude you from trials; but the joy and assurance and confidence you begin to build as a result of choosing to put Christ first in your life will change your life.

You will seek me and find me, when you seek me with all your heart (Jer. 29:13).

This verse in Jeremiah gives clear direction on beginning a relationship with Christ. It's in the seeking. Women do this well. When we are looking for the new lipstick of the season or hunting for those crazy cute boots people will rave over, we seek with great determination. We seek until we find and conquer, and then we literally tell everyone we know where we scored the treasured find and how much it cost.

We must seek that much more for the eternal. The temporal things bring satisfaction for a second, but the eternal, spiritual finds bring joy for a lifetime. God tells us that when we seek Him will all our heart, we will find Him. We are 100 percent promised that we will find Him. This is one of the promises we can claim if we choose to. Finding God is a choice.

Reclaim

He has granted to us His precious and magnificent promises, so that by them you might become partakers of the divine nature, having escaped the corruption that is in the world by lust (2 Pet. 1:4).

I am convinced that our nation is in a moral toilet because we as Christians have gotten lazy with God. One hundred percent of the promises in the Bible are at our fingertips and at our disposal; and if we were all partaking and claiming those promises over our nation, our marriages, our families, our circumstances and our leaders, we would not see abortion as an accepted choice; we would not watch our young women so desperate for acceptance that they starve themselves to the point of death; we would not experience our young men addicted to porn because they are desperately searching for something that only a relationship with Christ can bring.

God placed you on the earth to fight against the rule of the enemy. He needs you, no matter what your background, to accept His call on your life and begin or continue to cultivate an intimate relationship with Him. He needs you to act as Jesus to the world. The world needs the Jesus in you to tell them they are more precious than they could ever imagine because God sent His Son into the world to forgive and save them.

The action to reclaim is one that will take effort. It is not an easy thing to decide after habitual patterns have been formed to choose to do something outside the norm; but if you do so choose, true wealth is at your fingertips—not just monetary wealth, but also the wealth of the secrets of the Most High. It's the warrior stance of a Christian, with the objective of reclaiming all the promises that have been stolen from you by the lies of the enemy. Your intimacy with Christ will always require reclaiming the ground He has won in you.

My husband and I have faced dark trials, such as court battles with family members and severe financial woes. We have endured layoffs and rejection of the utmost kind. We have taken care of severely sick family and endured sickness ourselves, all the while claiming the promises of the Lord for peace.

> You keep him in perfect peace whose mind is stayed on you, because he trusts in you (Isa. 26:3, *ESV*).

Peace is a promise. When I decided to abandon *my* way, which led me to destruction, and accept this promise of peace, even in the most brutal of circumstances God calmed my soul. I survived because of peace.

Scripture tells us:

> But without faith it is impossible to please Him, for he that comes to God must believe that He is and that He is the rewarder of those who seek Him (Heb. 11:6).

Revive

After you have reviewed your spiritual state and reclaimed your ground and are in good standing with God, it's time to revive. One of the definitions of "revive" is "to restore the validity or effectiveness of." Restoring your effectiveness is a powerful place to be. When you are in God's Word, receiving wisdom for your personal callings, and you are praying in faith and believing and claiming the promises of Scripture, God uses you as an unstoppable force. Just like the dead brought to life, you will be able to gain confidence in the leading and guiding of the Holy Spirit. The Holy Spirit was given to us as Jesus promised when He ascended into heaven (see John 14:16-17) and is active in many different ways in the Christian walk (see John 15:7-10).

> The Spirit of God, who raised Jesus from the dead, lives in you. And just as he raised Christ from the dead, he will give life to your mortal body by this same Spirit living within you (Rom. 8:11, *NLT*).

As a believer, the very Spirit of God lives inside of you. Wow, drink that in! The almighty Spirit of God is given as a gift from God to guide and direct you. If you listen to and obey the promptings of the Spirit of God, even if they feel crazy, you will witness miracles.

This happened to me when I was flying to L.A. to do our first Blush conference there. I had my eyes closed and was heavy in prayer and I had worship music blaring in my ears. My prayer was strong and direct: *God, tell me what You have for our team this weekend.* I had felt uneasy about this conference for several months. God had given me a direct order to go to Los Angeles, but I knew that this specific conference would rock our team.

I paused in prayer a minute to wait for a reply. All of a sudden in my spirit I saw a picture of a young Latina girl with cornrows in her hair and wearing black wire-rimmed glasses. Picturing this in my mind, God said, *She will come with a group from a rehab center and she will be demon possessed.* I immediately sat up and opened my eyes only to see a brand new intern beside me. I knew that if I shared what I had seen it might freak her out, so I closed my eyes and kept praying.

When we landed in L.A. all I could picture was this young woman. The next two days I waited anxiously for the opening of the conference. The conference started and there was no sign of the girl. About halfway through the day I walked to the back of the auditorium to listen to one of our new speakers. I don't often get to hear the speakers, but this particular day I had that opportunity.

Skimming the audience with my eyes I stopped short when I saw a young Latina girl with cornrows in her hair and wearing black wire-rimmed glasses. I left the room immediately and notified a member on my team to not let her leave until I got a chance to talk to her.

I took the stage for the last session and I could feel the presence of the Lord thick in the room. I preached as passionately as I could, tears streaming down my face, as I pictured that young Latina girl. I offered an altar call and there were hands raised all over the audience as participants committed their lives to Jesus. The hands were a beautiful sight, but there was one hand that wasn't raised: that of my young Latina girl.

I was told backstage that there was a girl who left while I was speaking and ran to the bathroom and locked herself in a stall. My team couldn't get her to come out because she was convulsing. When I heard this, I knew exactly who it was. Eventually they were able to bring the girl to me backstage. She was the young Latina girl with cornrows in her hair and wearing black wire-rimmed glasses— the one God had shown me. She was convulsing and telling me she wanted to leave. As I tried to speak to her, I could tell that she was very uncomfortable. I stopped trying to talk to her and, with all the faith I had, I prayed and commanded the demonic influence to leave her. At the end of my prayer she was sitting in front of me, calm and peaceful.

We talked for a very long time and she shared that she was addicted to meth and had sold it on occasion. I asked her if she wanted to begin a relationship with Jesus. It was incredible to watch as she prayed to receive Christ as her Lord. She had come into the conference shaking and was now leaving the conference smiling and laughing.

This young girl's changed life is an example of what intimacy with Christ is all about. If I hadn't listened to the Holy Spirit, I wouldn't have heard about this girl and she would probably still be in bondage.

There is nothing else that compares to a strong, intimate relationship with the Lord. Our culture dismisses it as useless. But, Christian friend, understand that your life will in no way represent all that God has for you without intimacy with Him. The key to unlocking who you are is found in an intimate relationship with the Lord. No one can teach you how to perform it; you must do the work necessary to achieve it. A complex, deep, intimate relationship with our God begins with something as simple as seeking. And what a God you seek. Here are a few verses that speak to His might and supremacy:

When my enemies turn back, they shall fall and perish at Your presence (Ps. 9:3, *NKJV*).

The earth shook; the heavens also dropped rain at the presence of God; Sinai itself was moved at the presence of God, the God of Israel (Ps. 68:8, *NKJV*).

The mountains melt like wax at the presence of the LORD, at the presence of the Lord of the whole earth (Ps. 97:5, *NKJV*).

QUESTIONS THAT SEEK TRUTH

1. Did anything in my opening story resonate with your life? Explain.
2. When you think of the Lord, what characteristic do you associate most with Him?
3. In what way has my experience challenged your view of God?
4. Review your spiritual life. When was your last experience with God where you truly sought Him?
5. What excuses have you made about your lack of a close relationship with the Lord?
6. The relationship Jesus had with God the Father is a perfect example of intimacy. As Christians, we have access to God just like Jesus. Do you see that type of intimacy as attainable for you? What would you need to do to change your answer?

7. The intimacy level you have with God is based on your effort, not His. He is standing at the door of your heart knocking. Take some time right now and open the door to communion with Him. What did you pray?

8. If you followed the suggestion in question 7, what did the Holy Spirit say to you in your thoughts or in His Word?

9. What could you change about your calendar to make time with God a priority?

10. Fight for intimacy with Christ. What habit patterns do you need to alter in order to make room for your relationship with Him?

The Significance of Correction

*I'm sure I am significant, but my head knowledge and heart
knowledge are not coinciding. No, I don't deeply believe that I am
significant or will have a deep impact on the Kingdom.*

BLUSH ATTENDEE

**Can you see how God's correction of your direction
indicates that you are significant?**

Guess what? You are not perfect, and you sometimes need to be corrected. Personally, I shudder at the word "correction." I always want to be right. When my flesh grips me, I tend to believe that I always am right. As much as that would be amazing, it will never be true.

Most people struggle to a great degree with the subject of correction. Who wants to be corrected? Isn't it ironic then that we have a God-given desire to help all who are in need, and we love to run to the aid of any situation and add our two cents to save the world? Sometimes I think that if the president of our country would just call me, I could totally help him out. Well, that has never happened. As much as we may think we have it all figured out, we never will.

Correction is necessary for spiritual growth. In fact, it must happen if we are to grow! Because of our sin nature, there is no way we can know all that God has for us without being corrected along the way. The question of correction is not *if* we need it; it's *when* we need it.

There is a way which seems right to a man, but its end is the way of death (Prov. 16:25).

Most of us know that we must be corrected at some point, but it is a reality that is hard to accept. Even though we may know we need to change, when the change is forced on us, we fight it.

No matter the type of childhood home you grew up in, whether it was a home with heavy discipline or no discipline at all, God's Word tells us that He loves us too much not to guide us; and sometimes that guidance will be shown through correction. Let me say this clearly: Correction from God is not mean! God's correction always brings forth repentance, because His correction is love. A mindset that believes God is a bully and waits for us to fail so that He can zap us with His superpowers is just wrong thinking. Satan may work on us to think this, but if that is your mindset about God, it is not the truth.

My son, do not despise the chastening of the LORD, nor detest His correction; for whom the LORD loves He corrects, just as a father the son in whom he delights (Prov. 3:11-12, *NKJV*).

As a parent who loves my children, I correct them often to help them grow and mature. When I lovingly correct them, they always learn and are grateful for the correction. It was God's idea to correct our children lovingly so that they will learn. Since we are God's children, the reason God corrects us is because He is desperately in love with us! God's correction is not to humiliate or embarrass. His reason for correction is to maximize our lives. He wants only the best for us, and He wants us to partake in the riches of His glory.

If you are wallowing in sin, He can't do that. When you change your perspective on correction from something that is mean and hateful to something that is necessary to achieve God's biggest dreams for your life, it doesn't sound so bad, does it?

I was lying on the king-sized bed my parents had given Eddie and me for our wedding, feeling sick as a dog. Just a couple of months earlier I had found out after just a few months of marriage that I was pregnant with my daughter Grace. We were so excited! I remember taking about five pregnancy tests to be sure, then I called Eddie and said, "You need to come home. I have something to show you." He replied, "There is no way I can come home right now; what is going on?"

I couldn't hold it in any longer and blurted, "I'm pregnant, hah." I don't know where the "hah" came from, but I wanted him to know that my information was important. I remember that he paused for a moment and then began to scream. You could have heard us for miles, screaming and shouting from excitement. That was one of the greatest days of my life.

Under the Rod of God

Shortly after finding out I was pregnant, I became sick. I was not just morning-sickness sick, but really sick. I remember on average throwing up about 12 times a day. I couldn't eat, and I couldn't watch TV because the motion would make me sick. I couldn't go outside because for some strange reason the outdoors smelled to me; I couldn't touch or smell Eddie, because his very scent made me throw up immediately. Eddie couldn't eat in the house, so he bought a little grill he would use to grill food in the garage.

I know this sounds crazy but, trust me, every word is true; I was so sick that for about five months, I was completely bedridden. Eddie and I, back then, couldn't afford the anti-nausea medication I desperately needed, so I had no choice but to suffer. I ended up losing about 30 pounds. It was, to date, one of the most horrific things I have ever experienced.

I began to slip into a state of depression when the people surrounding us would ask Eddie if I was faking the sickness. I was isolated, scared and completely helpless.

Just a few months earlier, Eddie had been hired at a church in Indiana. He was their junior high pastor, and it was the first time he had been on full-time staff at a church. The pressure of his work responsibilities coupled with my sickness in the first year of our marriage made life extremely difficult.

After Eddie was hired at this particular church, and before I was pregnant, I remember him coming home and telling me his ideas for growth and advancement for the ministry. He would talk excitedly, gushing about all the things he would do to show Jesus to the junior high kids. I remember that I added every little piece of advice I could. He would talk and then I would interject a comment that I thought was brilliant. I would constantly tell him how to make his ideas better. I thought I was doing him a great service.

After every idea I offered, I would think, *Man, that was good.* Pride crept into my heart and I began to believe that Eddie needed me to have a successful ministry. It was a lie, but I believed it as truth.

After getting sick while pregnant with Grace, I became completely helpless. The strong woman who emerged after divorcing my first husband receded to the point of literally needing everything done for me. I remember Eddie brushing and washing my hair because I was too weak to do it. At times, I couldn't even stand erect. He would come home at night and paint my toenails to make me feel better.

My husband's servant attitude toward me during that time began to preach to me. I remember crying out to the Lord one day on that king-sized bed, asking the Lord why He wouldn't heal me and make me better. I shouted, "Why are You doing this to me? All I want to do is serve You." Like a tornado wind, the Lord's voice of correction spoke, saying, *Autumn, don't be so prideful as to think I cannot work without you.*

I lay in that bed under the rod of the Almighty's correction. I knew that He was speaking clearly to me and that the isolation and sickness were something I needed to realize was by God's grace and that He chooses to use us, not because of us but because of Him.

When I heard Him speak to me that day, I was changed. I have never been the same since. I needed to hear Him speak to me in such a way on the subject of pride that I would never forget it.

To this day, even though that was almost a decade ago, I think back to the voice of the Lord showing me that at any moment He has the strength to remove us from our pedestal of self-importance. That moment is a memory stone in my mind, and I believe it is one of the most loving things God has ever done in my life.

If God hadn't spoken so clearly and had let me continue in the mindset that I was irreplaceable, the fruitful years of ministry

God had for my life never would have happened, because God is not going to share His glory with anyone. He is the only one who deserves glory.

Correcting my path proved that God loved me too much to let it continue. As much as I wanted to be made well, God wanted my mind to be healed from the corruption of sin so that I could continue working effectively for Him.

Let's Get Real

I believe that correction is one of the things missing in modern-day Christianity, yet it's one of the most profitable things that could happen to any of us. I know that it is incredibly awkward to have a conversation with a friend about her sinful habit or thought process, but it is also one of the most loving things you can do for that person. In Scripture, we find a perfect example of correction in the book of Revelation, chapters 2–3. I believe there is a pattern of correction there that we can learn from.

John was the author of the book of Revelation. He was told by God to write a book of what God had allowed him to see and send it to the seven churches that were named Ephesus, Smyrna, Pergamum, Thyatira, Sardis, Philadelphia and Laodicea. Now, please stay with me. These were actual churches that existed, and these messages were written to them. Evidence has proven that they struggled with the exact things God challenged them with. Although these letters were written for these specific churches, I also believe they represent the different states of the Church today. Furthermore, we, as individuals who make up the Church, can glean all the principles for our lives.

It seems like God is having a conversation with each church, but the process is the same each time—different content but same method.

God Identifies Himself Personally

In each of the messages, God identifies Himself differently. He does not say, "What's up? It's God; let's chitchat." He represents Himself in a way that would emotionally make sense to the church.

For example, to the church of Smyrna, He identifies Himself as "The first and the last, who was dead and has come to life," knowing that this particular church would face martyrdom. Now, that is quite a personal look at how the church may have seen Him.

When God wants to correct us, He lovingly presents Himself in a way that would make sense to us. That way is different for each person. God may use many different avenues to get your attention—your pastor, a friend, your spouse, a sermon, a devotional reading, your small group. In these avenues, He will present Himself with whatever characteristic you identify with the most to gain your attention.

God Commends the Good Deeds First

With these churches, God commended five of the seven for their good deeds first and then made sure they knew that He was aware of all the positive things they had done. For example, He tells the church of Thyatira, "I know your deeds, and your love and faith and service and perseverance, and that your deeds of late are greater than at first" (Rev. 2:19). I love that He does this. I don't know about you, but before I get dealt some correction cards, I'd like to know that God sees what I am trying to do for Him.

Not only does He commend, but He also commends specifically. He usually does this through an unexpected source that points out things to you that he or she feels are effective for the Lord. I don't know about you, but there are several people whom I respect. This year for my birthday, I got a card that I will never throw away; it was from the two people in my life whom I respect the most, and inside the card they wrote an incredible message. I was so honored to receive this card that I got teary-eyed when reading it. It was an honor to be encouraged by this couple.

Only a loving God would point out that He personally sees our efforts for the Kingdom. God, in His love, shows us grace before He brings correction. He strides out with us as our great cheerleader; but when we don't catch on to the weaknesses in our character, He steps in because His name is at stake. Seeing this method makes all who believe that God is a mean God of judgment understand that although judgment is part of His character, He is the great leader of grace.

God Specifically Corrects

When God convicts of sin, His goal is correction. In each of these churches God is very specific with the commendation, but He is also very specific with His correction.

God is not interested in your repenting of sin you do not commit. Therefore, He is specific when it comes to correction. There was one such time this year when I thought I was doing everything as best as I could, but God got my attention and told me, "Surrender." Looking back, I realize I'd had angst in my spirit for a couple of months and couldn't put my finger on why. Finally, just like He spoke to these churches, He spoke to my heart and told me specifically what the block was. When it was pointed out to me, I was then able to repent.

You've Lost Your First Love

I love that God is direct. To the church of Ephesus, in Revelation 2:4, He plainly tells them they have lost their first love, which was God Himself. I see this happening all over the place. I see Christians lose the vigor and passion for the Lord they had when they first surrendered their life to Him. It is so easy after the initial excitement of salvation wears away to substitute work for God for a relationship with God.

Have you ever had a conversation with a prominent church member and all they do is talk about what job they are doing in the church and never actually speak about God Himself? We have become so busy spending our time working for God that we have forgotten who God is. God is not after amazing productions and organization; He is after your heart. His perfect plan is to have a love affair with you. If we are not careful, we can all fall under this category.

Wouldn't it be a tragedy to get to heaven and find out that you barely even know God, and all you had done was a bunch of work for a stranger?

You've Allowed False Teaching

To the church of Pergamum, God wanted to correct the fact that they were allowing false teachers in their church and teachers who were allowing the believers to compromise with worldliness. This is huge for us today.

We cannot compromise with worldliness. Our broken world doesn't need us looking just like them; God says that He has set us apart, and yet we do not really believe this. Let's talk about sex for a moment.

Abstinence before marriage is laughed at in most circles, including the church. I had a conversation with a devout Christian not long ago about this very topic, and when I brought it up, she got uncomfortable and said she was going to let her kids make the decision on whether to have sex or not.

I stood there and thought, *Huh? Why are we letting our culture dictate our moral compass rather than seeking God's outline for it and following that?* The truth is, we are allowing things on our TVs and computers at home that are completely against anything God would accept for His set-apart people. We run to our celebrity news channels far more often than we run to the Word of God. This has to stop.

I want to speak specifically to you. The idea of acceptance is great, to a point, but you cannot allow it to water down the message of the Lord. Going soft on issues in your family that God is clearly against calls for correction.

No doubt, God is frustrated by the amount of the world we let in to influence us where He wants to be our primary influence. Taking a stand against overwhelming worldliness at work, school or even in your home can literally be what God is asking you to do.

You've Tolerated Improper Leadership

To the church of Thyatira, God addresses the fact that they have tolerated a woman named Jezebel who calls herself a prophetess. She is charged with leading some astray with teaching immorality and the allowance of eating food sacrificed to idols. Now, it's interesting to me that a woman like this was allowed to have so much power in a church that was commended for some amazing things.

Let me speak to all my ladies for a second. As a strong woman myself, I adore you. But I would challenge you to look at yourself. If you are in any type of spiritual leadership, it is imperative that you lead well. Satan wants nothing more than for you to lead your flock astray. This can happen when you indulge in complaining, backbiting the other leadership, gossiping and always needing to be in control. You are not allowed, sweet woman, to bend the rules to suit your agenda.

I have had guests at our conferences who were sharing their talent express amazement at the unity of The Blush Network team. Our team is made up mostly of women. On more than one occasion, I have been complimented for the way we work together. We have heard that a unified, predominantly female team is rare.

The culture on The Blush Network team is to praise strengths and understand weaknesses. What kind of leader would I be if I allowed our team to be divided and didn't handle sin when it reared its head? Be aware, sweet friend, that you must not tolerate immorality in any form. If you have a leadership position, lead in a manner that the Lord commends.

You Are Spiritually Dead

Sardis is the next church God speaks to. I'm going to warn you, this is a harsh one, but important. He tells the church of Sardis that they are Christian only in name and that they are dead. He literally tells them to "Wake up" (Rev. 3:2). You may want me to stop with all the correction, but when I read about this church, my heart hurt. This church was a church that looked beautiful from the outside; there was no trouble in this church to speak of, and they were affluent and seemingly happy. Then God hit them with the words, "You are dead."

How sad it would be to think you are alive in Christ but you have never met Him. Could Satan trick us that much to make us believe that we are a child of the King, and yet we have never met Him? I fear this is happening with individuals all over the country. I do believe that we are going to be shocked when we get to heaven and see who is there.

Playing the church game doesn't get us into heaven; you can lead a small group or plant a church and not even have a relationship with Jesus. This is why I do what I do. I have led salvation messages at churches and Christian universities with almost unanimous response from the audience for salvation. Just because spiritual things surround you does not mean you have the Holy Spirit inside of you.

If you are reading this and don't really know if you have become a child of God, I ask you now to confess your sin and believe on the name of the Lord and invite Him into your life (read Rom. 10:9-10). *Now* is the time to wake up.

You Are Indifferent to God

The last correction in the book of Revelation goes to the church of Laodicea. This is probably the most well known of the churches due to the correction.

> I know your deeds, that you are neither cold not hot; I wish that you were cold or hot. So because you are lukewarm, and neither hot nor cold, I will spit you out of My mouth. Because you say, "I am rich, and have become wealthy, and have need of nothing," and you do not know that you are wretched and miserable and poor and blind and naked (Rev. 3:15-17).

Um, wow—I'm speechless. Can you imagine getting that letter? God takes great offense when people who have the Lord in their life don't care. They value their cars more than their Jesus. They get their designer jeans but forget about their salvation. They are sipping their wine and forgetting about the Living Water. God speaks so graphically as to say that He will spit them out of His mouth. Of all the pictures of God, I'd have to say that this is one I haven't pictured—God spitting. The very image is disturbing. It begs the question, is He the harshest on this type of church because this is the most common problem?

Imagine your children looking you in the face after you have sacrificed something enormous for them and you hear them say, "Who cares?" They see your very sacrifice as irrelevant. This is how the Christian represented by the church of Laodicea sees the sacrifice Jesus made on the cross. Material worth is much more exciting than eternal life. I fear this type of Christian is more common than you think, and if this is you, I ask you to pray for hunger for the Word of God. Understand that wealth can be taken at any time, but a relationship with Jesus cannot. Revive your desire for your Lord. He has a significant plan for your life, but He will not tolerate complacency.

God does not correct the churches of Philadelphia and Smyrna. In these two churches, He chooses to encourage them. Both are working hard for Him and have seen great difficulty because of it. In reading the text, we see that these two churches faced the most severe trials. Smyrna was encouraged to stay obedient until death and warned that they would face it.

God speaks so lovingly to Philadelphia because even with their "little power" they have kept God's Word. I love God's encouragement to the church of Philadelphia:

> I know your deeds. Behold, I have put before you an open door which no one can shut, because you have a little power, and have kept My word, and have not denied My name (Rev. 3:8).

The words "little power" minister to me. On many days, I have prayed, "Lord, I am just one person; how can I change the world?" The Philadelphians may have thought this as well. But the little power this church demonstrated got God's attention. It clearly states in Revelation 3:9-10 that He loved this church and would keep this church from the hour of testing that will come on the whole world. Their little power was not ignored or overlooked; it was encouraged.

Don't think for one moment that your influence does not gain the attention of your heavenly Father. We read in 2 Chronicles 16:9 that "the eyes of the LORD move to and fro throughout the earth that He may strongly support those whose heart is completely His." He is looking for little powers wholly devoted to Him to use in massive ways for His name. Wealth, intelligence and experience matter not to God; He is after the heart that belongs to Him.

I desperately desire for everyone to experience the riches of the Lord. He has radically changed my life, and I will spend my life passionately attempting to express it.

God Calls for Specific Action

After the Holy Spirit reveals sin, we must act in repentance. God tells these churches specifically, "Repent." God is serious about your repentance in every matter He reveals to you. To be a warrior for our King, we must not flake out when it comes to acting on the correction, which usually involves changing a habit. It's a difficult process to stop doing something that has become a habit. However, if God demands it, you have no choice if you desire to be in good standing with Him.

Sometimes, we don't have any idea that we have become wrapped up in a web of sinful habits until God reveals it. When God reveals, His grace has already been shown, and He is ready for you to shed the sin. He loves you too much to allow you to wade in the dregs of sin. He sees way more than that in you. Do you believe it?

Some stay wrapped up in a sin because they do not believe they can overcome it. The heavy accountability the Holy Spirit keeps on our souls when action is required is key to realizing significance. Without it, we cannot champion our life for Christ.

Responding to the correction of the Holy Spirit is the area where we tend to offer the most excuses. What would the world look like if it were excuse-free? Phrases such as "I'm too busy" or "I'm not strong enough" or "You don't know what I've done" are completely irresponsible and, quite frankly, God doesn't buy any of them. Victimizing yourself to others does not erase the demand for repentance. It's dangerous to throw out an excuse for not changing to the great God who overcomes.

I know, sweet friend, that to change an area of sin is almost debilitating, but it *is* possible. I have seen people who have been addicted to porn, to eating disorders, or who are suicidal, paralyzed by fear or laden with bitterness, repent and change completely. So get out of the dirt pit you are wallowing in and find true relief and promise in our great God.

All of our Blush Network conferences are unique. We never have one that is the same, and I suspect we never will. We boldly approach the throne room of the Lord before each conference and expect God to do what only He can do—convict and call to action. The emails pour in the days and weeks after we have left a city, telling us of success stories. Every story brings me to tears. These are stories where freedom has been found and true repentance has been realized. After each conference, my team will meet together throughout the day to hear the success stories and cry, knowing that God always moves.

At one of our conferences, I took the stage and saw that the audience was cold. I can read an audience almost immediately. I preached my heart out. I had a ton of notes that I knew God wanted to convey to the ladies. I was onstage for probably 20 minutes tops when I felt the Lord tell me to get off the stage. I was very confused. I had a ton more to preach and God specifically was telling me to get off the stage. I began to feel the words "You are done" in my spirit and it was almost like a flashing stoplight. The audience was pretty unresponsive to my message, so I wrapped up quickly and did just that. I left the stage puzzled but obedient.

The band came out to lead worship and I sat in the back telling the backstage manager what had happened. All of a sudden, the lights to the entire building went out. Immediately, I felt the power of God in the place. I took the stage again and challenged the audience on the power of God; and while I was speaking of His awesome power, the lights came back on and I was able to thank my powerful God for being faithful. Well, the room was completely silent. When the worship band came to finish us out, the spirit in the room had completely changed. Almost everyone in the room raised their hands in decision for our Lord.

God was right; I was done with my message, because He was ready to preach! To this day, my stage is God's, and anything He wants me to do, I will obey. At this particular conference, I received an email from a leader who was a part of the conference and who confessed to an addiction to pornography. Because the Spirit of God was so thick in the room, He convicted and challenged her to repent and called her to action, and she obeyed. Even the sin no one sees, God demands us to repent.

God Blesses the Overcomer

The last pattern we see God correcting in the churches is the promise of blessing if the church overcomes. Two of the promises were given to churches for overcoming trials, and the rest were given to churches that needed to overcome sin. Here is what each of these churches was promised:

Ephesus: "I will grant to eat of the tree of life which is in the Paradise of God" (Rev. 2:7).

Smyrna: "Will not be hurt by the second death" (Rev. 2:11).

Pergamum: "I will give some kind of hidden manna, and I will give him a white stone, and a new name written on the stone which no one knows except him who receives it" (Rev. 2:17).

Thyatira: "To him I will give authority over the nations; and He shall rule them with a rod of iron, as the vessels of the potter are broken to pieces, as I also have received authority from My Father; and I will give him the morning star" (Rev. 1:26-28).

Sardis: "Will thus be clothed in white garments; and I will not erase his name from the book of life, and I will confess his name before My Father and before His angels" (Rev. 3:5).

Philadelphia: "I will make Him a temple in the pillar of My God, and he will not go out from it anymore; and I will write on Him the name of My God, and the name of the city of My God the new Jerusalem, which comes down from out of the heaven from My God, and My new name" (Rev. 3:12).

Laodicea: "I will grant to him to sit down with Me on My throne, as I also overcame and sat down with My Father on His throne" (Rev. 3:21).

Wow! There isn't one of those things that I don't desperately desire. God gives the utmost jewels and heavenly treasure to those who make a definite choice to leave behind the wickedness of sin. He knows it is difficult, and He rewards those who battle to overcome.

I spent several years of my life wallowing in deep sin. I allowed sin to dictate my path, not realizing the amazing rewards that I willingly trashed. Do you know, sweet friend, that whatever it may be that you can't seem to get a handle on isn't worth it? Sin is fun for a season, but it's a quick season, and it is welded to severe consequences. One severe consequence is the forgoing of massive spiritual rewards, not only in heaven, but also those that are manifested on earth. No matter how deeply entangled you are in sin, now is the time to begin the process to overcome.

Let the Process Begin

What types of attitudes obstruct correction and indicate the need to stand up and do battle? I can immediately think of four: *pride, spiritual blockage, failure to listen, reluctance to repent.*

Pride Hinders Correction

We all need to go through times when we are forced to change. God normally uses trials to correct us. That's when pride can rear its head. Pride is one of the main reasons correction gets hindered. There are always things in our lives that the Lord wants to sharpen, and His Holy Spirit reveals where we have gone astray.

During that time in my life when I thought Eddie needed me to help him succeed, I didn't know that a prideful pattern had developed in my mind until God brought it to light. All I had noticed was separation from the Lord. I knew that something wasn't right; I just didn't know what was wrong. To get me back on the right track, the Lord brought me to a point where I would truly listen.

Spiritual Blockage Signals Needed Correction

Many times in my spiritual walk I have felt some sort of distance from the Lord. The Bible tells us that He will never leave us nor forsake us, but still there are times when I sense a spiritual block of some sort. One such day, I had felt this block for a month or so, and I was praying and asking the Lord to reveal what the blockage was. He simply said to my spirit, "You need to release anger." I meditated on that for several moments, which led to my writing a list of people's names toward whom I still held anger. To my surprise, there were 37 names on the list!

I cried and asked the Lord, name by name, to forgive me for holding onto anger for so long. Once I repented, the block I felt was gone. Justifying a spiritual block delays what God wants to correct in us.

Listening Engages Understanding

To truly reach your significance in Christ, you need to listen to His voice. Do you listen to Him? Or are you one of those people who just reads the Bible for 10 minutes once a week and calls it done?

I was asked this week how I listened to God. In this world saturated with distraction, it's easy to not listen. It is so easy to get on our smart phones or social media and drown out what God is trying to tell us. And sometimes, in our rebellion, we don't want to hear. God wants to speak to you, and you don't have to be freaked out about what He is going to say. But He does want to be your guide in this life.

God corrects us by bringing us to a place through some sort of difficulty or circumstance that makes us seek Him. He brings us to a place where all we have is Him, and then in His loving way, He speaks. When God speaks to our hearts about the issue needing attention, we then begin to understand the need for correction.

We don't serve a God that exists a million miles away; He is intricately involved in our lives, and He will speak to us when we will listen.

Repentance Restores the Relationship

King David is a prime example of a restored relationship with God through repentance. David had erred most definitely in His walk with God by having sex with a married woman and then having her husband killed. When the prophet Nathan came to David to confront him, David repented. His prayer in Psalm 51 is a beautiful depiction of a heart that is truly repentant. I'm sure that David, when it was all said and done, was very grateful for the Lord's correction.

King David serves as an example that correction is no re-specter of persons. If King David needed correction, we must see that we are not immune to correction; and we need to be aware that eventually we will need to bow under its rod.

A life that finds significance is one that is intensely seeking after the heart of God. Your surrender to the rod of correction will catapult you to the next level of intimacy with Father God.

QUESTIONS THAT SEEK TRUTH

1. What is your first thought about the word "correction"?
2. Proverbs 16:25 says, "There is a way which seems right to a man, but its end is the way of death." Is there a time when you were corrected and the act benefited you? How?
3. In the book of Revelation, God corrects seven churches. When God corrects, He does it lovingly. Is there a time when God corrected you and you changed? Describe it.
4. God corrects each of the seven churches in specific ways. Which church in Revelation does your attitude relate to the most?
5. When you correct yourself, God immediately blesses you. List a blessing you have received from godly correction.
6. Name a time when pride hindered you from changing. What happened after that?
7. If sin is present in your life, there will be a spiritual blockage with the Lord. Do you have a blockage right now? Describe what it feels like and what the specific issue might be.
8. Correction is significant because without it you cannot please God. How do you perceive correction after reading this chapter?
9. It's hard to listen when you get distracted. Take some time to focus, and search your heart. What do you think God is saying to you?
10. Correction produces intimacy with Christ. Pray that God will give you a sensitive and receptive attitude to His correction. Are you willing to be corrected?

5

The Significance of Prayer

Not a lot of people have made me feel significant.

If God says you are significant, wouldn't you agree that His desire to hear your prayers means there's no question about it?

Prayer has become a dead language to so many people. The day prayer was taken out of schools was the day that divine power was rejected by our culture. When we choose not to pray, we deny ourselves the right to the impossible. Seeing the impossible in our lives is something we all want, but secretly we have trouble believing it will happen. Well, prayer engages the spiritual realm, and if you aren't exercising your God-given right to pray, you won't see the impossible. If you don't pray, Christian friend, you are an ineffective Christian. The ineffective Christian is the one who denies the power of prayer.

Nothing spiritually significant will happen apart from prayer. Oh, you may see things that blow you away from a human standpoint, but you won't personally encounter God's treasure chest of impossibility made possible.

You can exist as a Christian without prayer, but you will be a powerless one, and Satan will take pride in you. My life would look totally different without prayer. This very book was prayed about for years before I ever met with a publishing company. What you are reading is not a book; it is an answered prayer.

At The Blush Network, our barometer for success is prayer. As a leader, I know that focusing on numbers and keeping up with other ministries are fleeting goals. Why would we ever try to do that? If I focused on other ministries and what they are doing, and I tried to keep up with them, I would be in a rat race that would end bitterly. However, if prayer is our foundation, and we are seeing our requests answered, I know that God is moving in our midst.

We have a prayer meeting every other Tuesday night at The Blush Network. We have been doing this for some time now, and in the time that we have been praying, we have seen all major personal prayer requests answered, and our ministry has exploded. One night in our prayer meeting, I looked at my staff and said, "Well, it looks like we need to come up with new things to pray for; God has answered all of our biggest requests." Prayers that our team had been praying for years were answered when we made prayer the focus of our ministry.

I get asked all the time, "How did you get into conference ministry?" Or "What tips can you give me for success?" When I answer, "Pray like your life depends on it, because it does," the questioner looks at me deflated and walks away as if that was the most ridiculous and unexciting answer I could have given. Let me just sum up the secret to any spiritual victory: prayer. The ones who walk away defeated make me think they have never fully experienced prayer. If you think prayer is boring, you haven't really prayed. If you think prayer is pointless, you haven't really experienced the miracle of answered prayer. I guarantee that if you have experienced Spirit-driven prayer, you make it a priority in your life.

Many years ago, I read the book *Fresh Wind, Fresh Fire* by Jim Cymbala. I dare say he mentored me without even knowing it. His desperate desire to see God move in spite of him or his circumstances resonated deeply with me. Looking at the reality of my circumstances back then, as a 22-year-old divorcée who had been rejected by my church and had absolutely no money or influence, I knew that to accomplish a huge dream, prayer was my only option.

After meeting the power of the Almighty while I was married to my first husband, all I did was pray from an attitude of desperation. My face was constantly planted on the floor of that small ranch house's back room, and I would sob for the Lord to move. I didn't have any special formula; all I knew was that if God didn't move, I didn't know what my future held. I hadn't gone to Bible school at that point, and I didn't know the Hebrew and Greek of any Scripture passage; but I did know Jesus. I wasn't intimidated by my lack of Bible education. I simply took the Bible for what it said. I thought if God said, "Ask and you shall receive," I sure wasn't going to be the moron who didn't ask. Sounded simple enough, so I did just that.

> In that day you will not question Me about anything. Truly, truly, I say to you, if you ask the Father for anything in My name, He will give it to you. Until now you have asked for nothing in My name; ask and you will receive, so that your joy may be made full (John 16:23-24).

I began a new phase of my spiritual life when I began to fully engage in prayer. Oh, I had prayed before, but my prayers were meaningless, with no conviction, and there really was no belief to back them. Therefore, I had concluded that either praying didn't work or God didn't want to answer my prayers.

When my then husband was home, it was difficult to go someplace quiet to pray. I began walking at a cemetery to escape my house. I know it sounds super morbid, but for some reason, that prayer venue wasn't crazy to me then. Maybe I was too messed up to realize that I was comforted by it rather than freaked out. I needed a place to get with the Lord and cry out to Him, a place where I wouldn't feel uncomfortable; so, to the cemetery I would go, and I would walk and pray.

I would usually go before sunset. Although, it didn't weird me out walking during the day, nighttime in the cemetery did seem strange. I would park at the beginning of the cemetery and do some stretching; and then, with my favorite tennis shoes on, I would begin to walk. The stillness and the aged oak trees with the statues of Jesus all over the garden made for the perfect walk.

The first couple of times I went, I would quickly pray and get back to my car; but the more I went, the more solitary communion with the Lord was something I had to have. It seemed to trump every voice. I began to listen to what I felt like He was telling me. I began to hear His voice to me. The more my confidence grew in Him, the more I began to do what He told me to do. I began to do little things, like encouraging someone or helping out with something. Even though my circumstances didn't change, I began to grow.

All my life I had heard that I was supposed to pray, but praying because you know you are supposed to is different from praying because your life depends on it. God graciously began to answer my small prayers. I was so excited every time He did. To me, seeing God answer a prayer was like Christmas morning. I began to fast and pray. Even though I was raised in a Christian home and I knew about the practice of fasting, I had no idea why anyone would ever do it. It sounded ridiculous to me. But I started to fast. The more I fasted and prayed, the more God actively answered my prayers.

I started asking for things that mattered, such as finances. When God came through on that, I decided to go for the big one. I knew I had chosen to marry the man I was married to out of plain rebellion to the Lord, but I had changed, and I now needed God to save me from it. I didn't know what God would think of my praying for His help on a sinful decision, but it seemed that He began to constantly answer my prayers; and I prayed over and over, *I have nothing to lose. Help me in this marriage.*

Help me, help me was my most common callout to the Lord. For a time, God seemed to be silent in that area of my life. However, He began to reveal my strengths to me. I had no idea who I was or what I was created to do, but God began to put on my heart a huge burden for women who were secretly suffering.

Through some activities at church, God revealed that I had leadership ability. I started speaking at local church youth groups about the Lord, and it always seemed to go well. So I began to pray for my future and in what capacity God wanted to use me. The more I prayed, the more the Lord built my desire to minister to women. The foundation for The Blush Network was being prayed over in those tender years of my spiritual walk and I didn't even realize it. Passion for others became my desire. It seemed that living my life just for me no longer mattered. The only thing that made sense was living my life for Jesus. All I cared about was living for Him and doing exactly what He wanted me to do, no matter the cost.

Changing my perspective made the long days of my marriage more bearable. The insults that were hurled at me didn't seem to hurt as bad. My focus wasn't my pain, but God's glory. In heavy prayer and fasting, God seemed to speak.

At one point, my parents were planning a trip to Lynchburg, Virginia, to visit my brother and sister, who were in college at Liberty University. Although the trip was three months away, I knew God wanted me to go with them. At this point, I had separated from my husband three times, and after counseling, things were not improving. So I began asking him if I could go. "No" was the immediate answer I got each time I brought it up. So I prayed and would ask later, with a quick no for a response.

I had asked him almost every day from the time the Lord told me I needed to go without getting a favorable response. Finally, it was the day before my parents were leaving. In faith, I asked for time off from my three jobs. In faith, I had arranged for all my responsibilities to be covered. The only barrier was my husband's permission.

I remember being too nervous to ask him that day; I felt emotionally naked whenever I stood before him. That evening, I gained enough courage to ask him if I could go. Time stood still as I waited for his answer. "Do whatever you want," he replied. Hardly believing my ears, I said, "Well, I'm going."

With that, I packed and went to bed to get prepared for an early morning trip.

When I arrived in Virginia, my prayers for my future began to take shape. I began to realize that my passion for ministry was one that was shared by many at Liberty University. God seemed to illuminate and focus His plan for my life. I knew that I had to do ministry; I just didn't know how.

Ten days passed on that trip to Liberty. My brother, David, was a musician on a ministry team affiliated with the school, and he just so happened to have a concert the last night I was there. My parents and I arrived early to the concert, and the team was in need of someone to go buy some bottled water. I volunteered to go. I went up the street to the 7-Eleven and gathered as many bottled waters as I could.

I had been praying the entire trip for the Lord to show me the next step to take with my marriage. I had no idea what I was going to do. I walked toward the checkout, and as I was setting the water down on the counter, the Lord spoke to my spirit. *You don't have to do it anymore* sounded in my mind as clear as day. I knew it was the Lord and He had spoken about the one issue for which I had been seeking His help for some time—my marriage.

I stared into space for a minute and the guy behind the counter asked, "Ma'am, hello?" I quickly snapped backed to reality, paid for the water and got in my car to go back to the church, but not before I took a moment to process what God had just said to me. Was the nightmare I had been living truly over? Could it be that God was releasing me? Yes, God had spoken so clearly; I remember it to this day.

With that, I told my parents of my decision as I traveled back home to Indiana. Now, all I had to do was tell my husband. When we arrived back at my house, I knew the time was now. He wasn't home when I got there. So I planted myself on the couch in the living room and waited. I prayed the entire time, asking God to give me a sign. If he walked in and didn't acknowledge me when he saw I was there, I would know it was okay to move forward with divorce; but if he looked at me and welcomed me, I would know to wait for divorce.

I sat in silence for what seemed like hours. The house was quiet when, all of a sudden, the garage door opened. I froze as I heard his footsteps walk through the galley kitchen and stop right in my line of sight. He looked at me and made no comment. He started to go through the mail he was holding in his hand. My heart started beating rapidly as I waited for him to acknowledge my presence, but it wasn't happening. Time stood still as the Lord spoke to my heart and told me, *It's okay, and it's time.*

When he finally acknowledged my presence, I knew that God had honored my request. I stood up, and with all the courage I had, I told him, "It's over."

I walked out of the room that night knowing that although I had a tough row to hoe in front of me, God had moved. He had spoken to me through the Holy Spirit. If the Lord had not been so specific in answer to my requests, no one knows what my life would look like now. Prayer changed me; and to date, I credit that time in my life to developing the discipline and privilege of prayer in my life.

Let's Get Real

You couldn't survive without your blood. Well, prayer is the lifeblood to connecting with God. Your spiritual life will die without prayer. Prayer is not optional. If you want to live a life that is saturated in purpose, you must pray. If you haven't already become a person who prays, today is the day to start. It is not too late.

We live in a culture of instant gratification. Prayer seems to take too long, which is why I believe it is a dying language. When we want something, we usually go get it. We are spoiled and don't really have to wait long for anything, so we fill our needs rather than seeking God to meet our true needs. This behavior edits prayer from our lives.

God isn't intimidated by your timetable. He cares not about what an impatient culture demands, because He loves you. His desire is for you to love Him enough to seek Him, even if it is contrary to everything you hear from others. Get this: The mysteries of God are ours through prayer! Extraordinary things will happen when you pray. His pleasure is in a child who will lean solely on Him. As your Creator, He alone knows the exact answer to your deepest need or smallest desire.

Whatever it is, have you prayed about it? You can go through the physical act of praying and not pray. You can close your eyes and bow you head and mutter a lackluster monologue to God, but all you are doing is checking a box of obligation.

I want to focus on prayer that changes things—on prayer that if it was not offered the world would not see things happen as a result. The entire book of Psalms is prayer. If you need the example of a good prayer, look no further than that book. David's words in the psalms are honest and raw. He wasn't out to impress people or show them how much "Christianese" he knew. He was just a man who required communion with his God.

Prayer as the Most Aggressive Form of Action

A lack of prayer is destroying the Christian's power today. Prayer is one of the most effective and offensive weapons we can use against the enemy's attack on our purpose.

Wars have been won with prayer; people have been healed through prayer; Jesus brought Lazarus back from the dead when He prayed. In a world riddled with trials, prayer must be our daily food.

When you are presented with any sort of hardship, get your face to the ground and seek God's counsel. His is the only voice that matters when the walls of your life are caving in.

One of my favorite stories in the Old Testament is that of King Jehoshaphat. He was the king of Judah when he got word one day that the Ammonites, Moabites and Meunites were approaching to make war with him. Hearing this, as you can imagine, scared him. The great thing about his response is found in these two verses:

> Jehoshaphat was afraid and turned his attention to seek the LORD, and proclaimed a fast throughout all Judah. So Judah gathered together to seek help from the LORD; they even came from all the cities of Judah to seek the LORD (2 Chron. 20:3-4).

If three armies were after me, I'd be scared as well! Jehoshaphat, in that moment, had an option: He could focus his attention on the great multitude coming, or he could focus on the Lord. This passage clearly says that he turned his attention to seek the Lord. The king of Judah understood that he was powerless without the power of the King of kings. True power comes from requesting the supernatural to invade the natural. Jehoshaphat stood in front of the great assembly of people gathered as a result of the coming threat and prayed.

I can almost hear the trembling in his voice as he said, "O our God, will you not judge them? For we are powerless before this great multitude who are coming against us; nor do we know what to do, but our eyes are on you" (2 Chron. 20:12). Imagine the scene as the text says all of Judah was standing before the Lord, with their infants, their wives and their children. This evidently was a huge threat that got the attention of the entire nation. I'm sure the scene was beautiful to the Lord as He saw His children come before Him in reverence, acknowledging their need of His power. So God moved.

> You need not fight in this battle; station yourselves, stand and see the salvation of the LORD on your behalf, O Judah and Jerusalem. Do not fear or be dismayed; tomorrow go out to face them, for the LORD is with you (2 Chron. 20:17).

I can hear the entire nation of Judah cheering as this word was offered by Jahaziel. Imagine the relief that God had promised deliverance. True to His word, the next morning when the entire nation began singing praises to the Lord, the Lord set ambushes against the multitude that was against Judah; and when it was all finished, they had destroyed each other completely.

This is the result of prayer. Prayer, and the intent through prayer to see God move, ended in huge victory. Judah didn't have to raise one finger in combat, because the combat was the Lord's to fight. Our battles may be presented to us, but they have the name of the victorious Warrior attached. You face no battle that God won't win on your behalf. But you must turn your attention to seek Him.

The LORD is a warrior; the LORD is His name (Exod. 15:3).

Whatever the battle, assume the position of face to the ground in prayer and engage the Great Warrior.

Prayer Wimp or Prayer Warrior?

The more we realize our need for prayer, the more passionately we will pray. I used to pray like a wimp. (I feel annoyed just thinking about that!) I'd pray, "Lord, thank You for this day; bless everyone I know, amen." *What?* With prayers like that, why even bother to pray? Looking back, I realize I prayed just to say that I prayed.

It frustrated me that my prayers weren't getting answered, but now I know it was because there was no belief or passion behind them. Bottom line, I prayed simply because I believed simply. I really didn't know how much I needed God, because I felt like I was doing okay on my own. Then my life collapsed and my prayer life came to life. I began to pray actively, not passively. I began to understand that there was a God who is ready to work on our behalf, but He wants to be consulted. A robust prayer life indicates robust spiritual health.

David, in the book of Psalms, clearly understood the power of God to move on his behalf. He didn't offer wimpy prayers; he boldly presented God with requests because he understood he couldn't do what God wanted him to do without God's intention.

O God, You are my God; I shall seek You earnestly; my soul thirsts for You, my flesh yearns for You, in a dry and weary land where there is no water (Ps. 63:1).

Understand, sweet reader, you are in the position to commune with the Most High. If you had an audience with the president of the United States and could ask for his power and help at any time, I'm sure you would do it. Our God gives the president his power. Yet, we don't approach Him as such. We have permission to approach God in a bold fashion. Bold purpose should produce bold prayers.

So let us come boldly to the throne of our gracious God. There we will receive his mercy, and we will find grace to help us when we need it (Heb. 4:16, *NLT*).

Your wimpy prayers don't get results because there is not much to answer. When calling on the name of the Lord, who is capable of anything, why waste your breath with nothingness. Prayer warriors do not have to be defined only as the older ladies at church; you can be a prayer warrior. Act as if you have the power of the Almighty at your immediate access.

Pray Specifically

She, greatly distressed, prayed to the LORD and wept bitterly. She made a vow and said, "O LORD of hosts, if You will indeed look on the affliction of Your maidservant and remember me, and not forget Your maidservant, but will give Your maidservant a son, then I will give him to the LORD all the days of his life, and a razor shall never come on his head" (1 Sam. 1:10-11).

Hannah's prayer is such a beautiful example of praying specifically. God had chosen to close her womb, and she was heartbroken because of it. She desperately wanted a son, and so that is exactly what she prayed for. She seized the opportunity and wasn't intimidated by the fact that the answer might be no. She prayed like a warrior for her son, and God blessed her with a son. In 1 Samuel 1:20, we read that Hannah "named him Samuel, saying, 'because I have asked him of the Lord.'"

How do you know if God is answering your prayer if you don't pray specifically? When God answers specific prayers, faith is strengthened. When you have a desire for something specific, God knows what your desires are. Asking for the specific desires of your heart is necessary in acknowledging that God would answer them. If you don't pray specifically, you won't get answered specifically. Prayers such as "Bless all the babies of the world" would be impossible to know had happened unless you knew all the babies of the world. However, if you choose to pray for a sick baby named Mike, and ask for complete healing, and God heals him, God has answered your prayer, and your faith will be encouraged.

I don't know about you, but I have way too much to do to waste time on blanket prayer. I have determined that I do not want to live my life without seeing the might of the Almighty; one way to do that is to pray specifically.

Do you worry that you will be disappointed in prayer? You may think, *What if I ask specifically and God doesn't answer me? I can't risk being hurt again.* Sometimes, we don't want to test God too much because we don't want God to let us down. When God doesn't answer the way we want Him to answer, we start believing that He answers everyone's prayers but ours. I want to tell you, that is exactly what Satan wants you to believe in order to keep you from praying!

Understand this: When you are praying that God will always answer according to His will and not yours, you don't know what you need or even what you want; and when you filter your desires and requests through a God who knows exactly what you need and want, He gives you an answer based on His knowledge.

When I started developing my prayer life, it seemed as if God answered all my prayers quickly. Then, as I grew in my prayer life, I was praying harder, but my prayers seemed to have a delay in the answer. For a while, that threw me. I didn't understand that while I was becoming more intentional and specific in prayer, my answers were delayed. In this phase of my prayer life, God was growing my dependence on Him. I now understand that He delayed answers for a time to flex my prayer muscle. He wanted me to go deeper, and seeking Him through prayer is the avenue for communion with Him.

Now I understand that no matter the outcome of my prayer, the answer is always in my best interests. He always answers, sometimes speedily, sometimes with a time delay; but He always answers. His timing and answers, I have learned, are always what are best for me.

The Blush Network was in year two of operations when it was becoming very clear that my team and I could not manage the growth. My husband, Eddie, had been a youth pastor for years and was helping us on the side with The Blush Network. Understanding the need, Eddie quit his job to help The Blush Network for a season.

I was overwhelmed when he told me, but my prayers immediately went to God's financial provision for our family. Eddie and I prayed like crazy and tried to think of all the options to have enough income that would let him help us out. I won't forget the day when I was on my elliptical, crying out to the Lord and asking Him to move soon. We had no idea what we were going to do.

A couple of days later, we received a call from a very unlikely source that made it possible for Eddie to work for The Blush Network full time. The call blew me away. I still stand amazed at God's provision. God provided more money monthly for us than any of the youth pastor jobs had ever provided. God went above and beyond because we dared to ask Him to provide a full salary for our family.

What is your exact need? That should be your exact prayer. Nothing less should be allowed or tolerated. God is a God of organization, detail and creativity. He understands getting things exact. Sweet friend, He will not put you to shame; it is against His nature.

Pray Things Through

Pray until God answers. I have learned to pray until I see the manifestation of my prayer. When you pray, you absolutely engage God. However, when God begins to work, most of the time you do not see it. There is a process to every prayer. Maybe it's praying for someone who has cancer to be made completely well. Well, if God begins to kill the cancer in that person's body, you will not see it until test results reveal that the person has been healed. Or if you are praying for a godly man to marry, and you have prayed over and over, you have no idea when your first prayer was prayed how God begins to move toward the full manifestation of that prayer. When you are standing at the altar with a godly man, your prayer has given birth to marriage.

While I was praying for God to give me opportunity to launch The Blush Network, I would get frustrated when it seemed He was ignoring me. I prayed for 10 years to launch The Blush Network. I knew that God had confirmed to me that this is what He had for me; but where was He? I would ask Him constantly, *Where are You, and why aren't You moving in this?* Yet, He was working all the time. He was preparing things behind the scenes perfectly to allow the launch of The Blush Network to be successful.

Looking back now, I see how the Lord worked each time I prayed. However, to complete the manifestation of my prayer He had to manipulate circumstances. He worked all 10 years, and because I tarried in prayer, we have a successful ministry. The only reason we exist is because God was answering my prayers even when I couldn't see it.

You must understand that even though you don't see the answer in two weeks, He is answering. You must set your sights on the unseen eternal things and not be so hung up on what you can see. Faith and prayer are buddies. Whether you believe it or not, God moves every time you pray. When you stop praying for a request because you haven't seen God move, you stop too soon.

Now He was telling them a parable to show that at all times they ought to pray and not to lose heart (Luke 18:1).

In this passage, Jesus tells a story of a woman who continually went before an unrighteous judge for protection. The judge was unwilling to do anything for a while, but because of the woman's continual and consistent request, the judge gave her protection.

And the Lord said, "Hear what the unrighteous judge said; now, will not God bring about justice for His elect who cry to Him day and night, and will He delay long over them?" (Luke 18:6-7).

This story preaches that we are to labor in prayer until our great God answers. Do not lose heart, my friend. God is working even now in your most earnest prayers. Don't give up; the answer is on the way.

Decisions Founded on Prayer

If you don't lay a foundation of prayer for the events and decisions in your life, you will be relying on your own strength—a big mistake. Laying the foundation of prayer before you make any big decision makes it subject to God's will. Surrendering your will and sacrificing your idea and desire to Him first please Him. Action without the assurance of God's presence behind you will result in catastrophe.

We see in the Bible that there are many accounts of men and women who sought God before they acted. In Exodus, we have the privilege of reading a beautiful example of a powerful prayer life. The interchanges between Moses and God are authentic, challenging and powerful. We look at Moses as such a pillar of Christian faith, but he was nothing but a Hebrew son who was willing to obey God. Through Moses' communion with God, miracles happened. He laid the foundation of prayer because he accepted clearly that without God he didn't have power. Seeking the Lord first allowed him to map the clear blueprint for you to follow.

Proverbs 16:9 tells us:

A mind of man plans His way, but the LORD directs His steps.

Foundational prayer is how God communicates with you the steps He wants you to take. In the book of Exodus, from beginning to end, Moses sought of the Lord direction for each move he made. From leading the nation of Israel away from the power of Egypt to crossing into the Promised Land of Canaan, Moses sought the Lord. One of my favorite verses, which I pray often, is one that Moses prayed out of desperation:

Then he said to Him, "If Your presence does not go with us, do not lead us up from here" (Exod. 33:15).

The awareness of failure without God's presence struck Moses to the core. It put him in such a fright that he would not continue without the Lord's leading.

I have prayed many times in the quietness of my talks with God for His presence. Without God's stamp of approval on what I do, I don't want to do it. It would just be a charade. I have learned the hard way, in living a life that was devoid of the leading of the Lord, and I have not the slightest desire to go back. My way led to destruction; His way has always brought me to greener pastures. In times of doubt while running the race God has placed me on, I can always take comfort in the fact that my journey has a foundation of prayer and God's direction to weather the storms.

If foundational prayer is not a habit of yours, start now.

Pray God's Word Back to Him

God loves His Word.

> For He spoke, and it was done; He commanded, and it stood fast (Ps. 33:9).

His Word is truth. When we accept His Word as truth and use it in the language in which we interact with Him, we bring Him glory.

> If you abide in Me, and My words abide in you, ask whatever you wish, and it will be done for you (John 15:7).

Using His words when speaking to Him gives evidence of the action of abiding. Whatever He promises in His Word we have the capability of claiming. The very idea of claiming a promise is praying God's Word back to Him. Many times in prayer I have reminded God of things He said were rightfully mine. Provision for my family's needs, grace to get through a trial, power to overcome satanic attack, are all promised through the very Word of God. Praying God's words back to Him is an expression of faith.

Jesus was speaking to the woman at the well when He said, "If you knew the gift of God, and who it is who says to you, 'Give me a drink,' you would have asked Him, and He would have given you living water" (John 4:10). Knowing that God's promises are our gifts to claim, and understanding who we approach when praying, unlocks the supernatural. I believe this practice not only brings God glory, but it also encourages us. Many times when I am praying, the Spirit will remind me of a verse, and therefore I repeat it. His Word is truth, and when I am reminded of truth it helps me to not wander from it.

Remember, no prayer equals no power.

QUESTIONS THAT SEEK TRUTH

1. Is prayer a dead or a living language in your life?
2. There's a difference between effective prayer and meaningless prayer. Effective prayer produces answers; meaningless prayer produces frustration. After evaluating your prayer life, how would you describe your prayers?
3. Your significance will demand your use of prayer. You cannot achieve without it. When have you stopped trying to go your own way and used prayer as your only weapon?
4. Exodus 15:3 says, "The LORD is a warrior; the LORD is His name." Having the Lord as a resource in any situation will always produce victory. When have you engaged Him as your Warrior?
5. If you do not pray specifically, you will not be answered specifically. What are three specific needs you have right now? Are you praying over them earnestly?
6. One of the biggest mistakes in praying is to give up too soon. Is there a specific prayer you have prayed for many years? Will you commit to see it through?
7. No significant act happens without foundational prayer. What do you want to see happen in your future that needs to be prayed about right now?
8. God loves His Word and identifies with it. Praying the truth of His Word produces answers. What promise in the Bible will you pray back to the Lord in faith and thanksgiving?

9. John 15:7 says, "If you abide in Me, and My words abide in you, ask whatever you wish, and it will be done for you." The principle of God's Word abiding in you is crucial to your significance; what passage of Scripture will you choose today to memorize so that it will abide in your heart? (It would be good to do this on a regular basis!)

10. Without prayer you will have no power. How have you seen this truth in your life? Are you already praying in power, or do you need to start developing a pattern of regular prayer?

6

The Significance of Trials

I'm not going to lie. I feel pretty stagnant.

BLUSH ATTENDEE

Would you believe trials are given to help you, and the end is great reward?

Why do we look so depressed when a trial enters our life? We are a victorious people whose inheritance is the power of God at work in our lives. That makes us champions before the battle even begins. So lift up your head!

I know you hate me right now for saying trials are no reason to get discouraged. That's because you're not yet aware that the amount of spiritual wealth you are gaining even while you read this could change your life. Your spiritual education is formed in the midst of a trial. Do you want your life to be stale? To stay business as usual? Without the sharpening that comes from trials, you will remain in the same stagnant state.

It is because of my trials that I am proud of who I am. Without them, I was defined by others' definition of me. Now I can proudly proclaim that I have learned where my true definition and acceptance lie; and that knowledge is because of the tremendous burden of the trials God has brought me through. Are they fun? *No!* Are they the best thing that could ever happen to you? Yes, because that is where the Lord's power is multiplied and made available to you.

Now, I am not living in a fantasyland, because I have faced harsh trials. However, what if we changed our perspective about trials, and rather than wading through suffering with depression, we waded through it knowing that trials give us the opportunity for victory?

> He sent from on high, He took me; He drew me out of many waters. He delivered me from my strong enemy, and from those who hated me, for they were too mighty for me. They confronted me in the day of my calamity, but the LORD was my stay. He brought me forth also into a broad place; He rescued me, because He delighted in me (Ps. 18:16-19).

There is no intimacy compared to that of the created with her Creator during a devastating trial. I have found the treasure of my Lord even while in the pit of despair. In the midst of the most debilitating news, conflict, suffering or journey, I have seen the Lord bow the very clouds of heaven and come to my defense. When the deterioration of self meets the strength of the Lord, the result is growth.

Trials are to be expected in this life. Their purpose is to gauge the spiritual temperature of your faith. Many times, when I have entered into a trial, I have been surprised at the amount of faith that I possess. I would even say that one cannot know the depth of his or her faith without the measuring stick of a trial.

In James 1:2, we read that we are to consider it joy when we encounter trials, because the testing of our faith will produce endurance. There is a great need to endure when following God's plan for your life. The call on your life will be surrounded by trials because your purpose will require faith. God's purpose for us is not something we can attain by ourselves; otherwise, we would not need God.

Are you in a trial right now? You can overcome it. That may not seem possible, but it is. Your mind, body and strength may say otherwise, but I am telling you right now that you are able to overcome your trial, and you can be victorious while under it. That trial is there to produce endurance in you; and endurance is not attained without a decision to rise above it.

> Blessed is a man who perseveres under trial; for once he has been approved, he will receive the crown of life which the Lord has promised to those who love Him (Jas. 1:12).

This idea of overcoming the greatest odds seems like an anomaly when there is no understanding that overcoming the greatest trial can be a regular occurrence for one who possesses the power of God. But factoring God out of your trial will make the trial end with defeat.

God will not give you a trial that you cannot overcome with His power. He promises in His Word that victory is attainable, because anything He allows in our lives we can overcome through Him.

> No temptation has overtaken you but such as is common to man; and God is faithful, who will not allow you to be tempted beyond what you are able, but with the temptation will provide the way of escape also, so that you will be able to endure it (1 Cor. 10:13).

I felt like I was in a trance as I started my 30-minute drive home. Both kids were snuggled asleep in their car seats unaware of the pressure Eddie and I were facing. News that the court battle with family members was going to be impossible for us to win deadened my mind to the point of numbness. I had no words to express my emotions, but the desert landscape around me seemed to reflect the state of my heart.

The past six months had been a nightmare. Eddie worked a full-time job as a youth pastor at a church in Chandler, Arizona, and I stayed at home with two very small children. That scenario would be enough to tax anyone's tranquility; however, God chose that spring for us to face some of the hardest trials to date.

Just a few months earlier, my husband received a call at four in the morning telling him to get on a plane and come to his hometown because his dad was in the hospital. The next day, Eddie and his brother made the difficult decision to take their dad off of life support. Still in shock, we were faced with the challenge of how to take care of Eddie's mom, as she had been diagnosed with some medical problems. Bob, Eddie's dad, had cared for her their entire marriage, and the need was for full-time help.

Our stepping in to care for her was met with resistance, but we knew what the Lord had told us to do, so we pressed forward. This action engaged one of the most tragic events in our life to date—an unwanted court challenge. This was a crushing blow while we were already dealing with the surprising passing of Eddie's dad. So we prayed and prayed, begging God to show us what steps we should take next.

God answered with His Word one night as I lay on my bed in a pool of tears. When my eyes caught the words in Psalm 37, I knew it was a word from the Almighty who had reached down in my despair that night. The Scripture passage comforted my broken heart and gave me a confidence that I didn't seem to have just 10 minutes prior. The life-giving passage reassured me of the path we should take, and to keep on. From then on I knew His power was with us. With His strength, we could be victorious in this mess, but only with His strength—mine was long gone.

Even when the situation got worse, we continued to move forward. We were in a battle that was not against flesh and blood, as the book of Ephesians says. We were in a battle against powers of darkness (see Eph. 6:10-12).

I was at my wits' end as I drove home that day. I wanted to give in and go back to just being a great mother to my babies and helping Eddie at the church. I didn't want to fight any longer. My fight was gone. Victory seemed such a long way away in the dark tunnel of impending defeat. All of a sudden, my mind seemed to be jogged to the night God gave me Psalm 37. It was as if I could taste the words from the passage encouraging me. Courage began to swell in my heart, and my mind snapped back from the clutches of the enemy to the triumphant realm of the Lord. I began to pray. I didn't pray a wimpy, passive prayer. I began to pray like my very life depended on every syllable uttered.

I remember staring at the mountains and straining my voice as loud as it would go as I offered desperate pleas to the Most High. I began to remind Him of that Psalm 37 passage and that we were only following what He had asked us to do. I felt a boldness running through my body, not one that I had produced, but a holy, supernatural, audacious passion for justice. In those moments, I knew that there was nothing I could do to change the situation, but I chose to believe that God could do anything to bring us through victoriously. My job was not to focus on my next move, but to focus on my valiant Warrior. I prayed very specifically in the car that day for God to show up in the next three days in a way that would turn the situation around, and I believed He would. 1/12/21

The next day was Wednesday, and I was getting my children ready to go to church when the Lord spoke to me and said, "Pack some clothes." I thought that was ridiculous, so I immediately dismissed the thought. I continued in the routine care for my children and felt a stronger prompting in my spirit: "Pack some clothes." Kind of looking around, I felt like Samuel when God was calling out his name in the middle of the night (see 1 Sam. 3:10). Not realizing the Holy Spirit was speaking to me, I again ignored the prompting. Again, I heard, "Pack some clothes." I rushed out the door and dismissed the thought once again.

Eddie and I and the kids were coming back from church that night when the phone rang. It was a family member saying we needed to come to Eddie's hometown because His mother had had an accident. So we went home and packed bags and left. When we arrived, God had orchestrated such an event that it swung the case in our favor and we ended up winning the court battle. God gave us victory.

Overcoming that ferocious trial was accomplished only when we stood in the face of definite defeat and believed that God was the God of the impossible.

Let's Get Real

God's Word says, "For nothing will be impossible with God" (Luke 1:37). Without engaging your faith, your trial will become a train wreck. However, when you exercise faith, you will have a front-row seat as you watch the miracles of God. When God allows trials, He wants to show you the great mysteries of His power that without question will increase your faith. When we have learned that we can overcome and that there are rewards for overcoming, I think it's much easier to navigate the trials in our lives. However, there are several pitfalls that can trip us up and keep our faith wimpy. You will need to champion these potential pitfalls as you navigate the faith path.

A Trial Does Not Mean God Is Mad at You

The enemy wants you to believe that God is mad at you when you are facing something that seems mean and unfair. God is not a villain. Quite the opposite is true. There is a difference between God allowing consequences for sin in your life and allowing trials. A consequence is a result of an unrepentant heart in a repetitious sin. A trial is allowed to purify us in our faith and to grow us in the Lord.

We read in 1 Peter 1:6-7, "In this you greatly rejoice, even though now for a little while, if necessary, you have been distressed by various trials, so that the proof of your faith, being more precious than gold which is perishable, even though tested by fire, may be found to result in praise and glory and honor at the revelation of Jesus Christ."

These verses compare the strengthening of our faith to something that is more precious than gold, because faith doesn't perish. The production of faith in your life is only accounted for by the trials you overcome. The suffering Job is a perfect example of that. Because Job was a godly man, God had blessed him.

> There was a man in the land of Uz whose name was Job; and that man was blameless, upright, fearing God and turning away from evil. Seven sons and three daughters were born to him. His possessions also were 7,000 sheep, 3,000 camels, 500 yoke of oxen, 500 female donkeys, and very many servants; and that man was the greatest of all the men of the east (Job 1:1-3).

The Bible calls him the greatest man in the east. That statement alone tells us of his status. All that a person could ever want, Job had; but that is not what defined Job. The very first verse in Job tells us not of his earthy wealth but of His character. The fact that the Bible mentions his character first shows us that Job's wealth was secondary to him. His wealth was significant to speak of because he lost it all. But that didn't mean that God was mad at him; God was pleased with Job.

Sometimes, suffering in the midst of God's blessing doesn't make sense to us; but clearly, Job represented such a character that it not only got God's attention, but it also afforded God an earthly example for us to benefit from today.

> The LORD said to Satan, "Have you considered My servant Job?
> For there is no one like him on the earth, a blameless and up-
> right man, fearing God and turning away from evil" (Job 1:8).

There it is, straight from the Lord's mouth: God handpicked Job to be tested. After Satan was through with Job, his kids had all been killed, along with all of his servants, all of the sheep, all of his camels; and his body was covered in boils. All this happened in the span of one day!

But isn't that the way it happens with us? We are walking along just fine, and then all of a sudden we start getting hit repeatedly with several horrible things. *Bam! Bam! Bam!* God knows the exact trials that we can stand under. He allowed such severe trials for Job because He knew of Job's fierce devotion and faith. God knew that if Job stood under the weight of the trials that were allowed in his life, millions upon millions of people over thousands of years would be encouraged. There was a plan for Job; it wasn't the Lord being mean to him; God was very intentional in the trials He allowed Satan to throw on Job because of the massive amount of comfort it would bring the human race if the trials were overcome.

Job's resolute decision that God is great no matter what is mind-blowing when you consider the circumstances he found himself in. His audacious trust in God is not just to be applauded but is also to be duplicated in our lives.

At the end of the book that bears Job's name, God blessed Job twofold. He gave him back more than he had in the beginning because Job had triumphed and did not forsake the Lord.

God looks at you today knowing your strength and all of your potential. I wonder if the trial you find yourself in would be more manageable if you knew that God has huge plans for the use of the wisdom you will gain during the trial? And He has a great number of people in mind whom you will encourage because you chose to overcome. Although you may not know the plans God has for your trials, He does.

Not one hurt is wasted, sweet friend; not one tear is shed without a powerful Master's plan for each one. God is just asking your faith to prove victorious in this season. He is not mean; He adores you and wants to use you to your fullest ability. That is the ticket to pure joy.

If Job knew at the time the kind of encouragement that mankind would receive as a result of his suffering deeply for a season, I can bet he would do it again. When we come through a season of trial and see the benefit in it, it is likely that we would, without a fight, choose to go through it again.

Removal of the Hedge Does Not Remove All Protection

After God suggested Job as a candidate for Satan's attacks, Satan responded almost in disgust:

> Then Satan answered the LORD, "Does Job fear God for nothing? Have You not made a hedge about him and his house and all that he has, on every side? You have blessed the work of his hands, and his possessions have increased in the land. But put forth Your hand now and touch all that he has; he will surely curse You to Your face" (Job 1:9-11).

The first question in this series of questions from Satan is, "Does Job fear God for nothing?" Here God has offered Job as a challenge for Satan to consider; and even though the supremacy of the Sovereign One spoke of Job's blamelessness, Satan rebuts the suggestion with finding blame. He accuses Job of following God due to God's blessings, and not out of love for Him.

I want to speak to that issue as it relates to you. If Satan stands before the throne of the living God and attempts to discredit each pure act of worship, he is also trying to get you to discredit yourself. If he can get you to voluntarily discredit yourself from offering an act of worship to the Lord, it's light work for him.

But when you push past the lies planted in your mind, Satan's labor increases.

My mind has been attacked with the most outrageous thoughts; some I would never pen due to their offensive nature. However, when a thought that seems barbaric toward what I know is true about my heart enters my mind, I recognize the origin and move it out. Just because I have a thought doesn't mean I have to believe it. We must be like gangsters in shooting down Satan's lies when they come into our thought processes. If Satan tried to get our King Jesus to believe something crazy when he tempted Him in the desert, his method will be the same toward you.

The second question Satan offers to the Lord is, "Have you not made a hedge about him and his house and all that he has, on every side?" This is where we get the idea of a "hedge of protection" that you may have heard about in church. I used to hear it all the time when I was growing up, and back then I had no idea what "hedge" even meant. One crucial thing to pull from this verse is that once you are a child of God, you have an enormous shield of protection over you. If there were not a hedge over you as a Christian, more than likely Satan would have killed you by now. Sorry to be that blunt. In the story of Job, we have proof of Satan's intentions without God's protection. God knows that we must have His protection to fight and not be overcome. No hair on our head is subject to harm with God's shield around us.

Some of us live in constant fear. Masses of people are plagued by anxiety. I, myself, have struggled with fear. Fear seems to hit at times when I am at a weak point. Fear is not fact; it is the impending thought of "what if?" When we factor God out of our circumstances, fear is a very real struggle. Things that the Lord can handle with ease cause us to get overwhelmed. I have been paralyzed by fear for no reason a few times in my life, usually in seasons of extreme weakness. In those moments when I let fear dictate its way, I have chosen to forget factual evidence that God's hedge of protection is guarding my very life. A God who blesses with protection guards the life that cultivates righteousness.

Second, God allows the hedge to be removed. With limitations, God allows trials to come into our lives. This is something no human would allow for him- or herself. When the hedge of protection is removed, God carefully monitors it. No trial is allowed that would defeat us, but only the trials that we have been equipped to overcome with the power of Christ. We may feel as if we cannot champion the test, but it wouldn't be allowed if God didn't intend to strengthen us during the process.

Because growth is necessary for anything to bear fruit, why are we caught off guard when God allows us the opportunity to grow? When we are tested to our limit, it is because a loving God desperately desires us to live a life of significance and not succumb to a life of stagnation.

I fear that too many Christians have given up under trials because exercising their faith in the midst of a trial seemed just too hard and they didn't realize that the miracle was on the other side of the hardest day.

When you give in to the pressure of a trial, you sacrifice the true victory that is yours to claim. Giving in just short of a miracle is a tragedy in the Christian life. You may not know until you get to heaven the rewards that had your name on them if you had just powered through.

Your Trial Has Limits

Job is a perfect example of suffering trials with a limit. After God gave Satan permission to try Job, He also gave Satan a limit:

> So the LORD said to Satan, "Behold, he is in your power, only spare his life" (Job 2:6).

Trials are only allowed when filtered through our Father God. Evil has no access to us except through the strainer of a loving Father. God's perspective and Satan's perspective on our lives are completely different. God wants to strengthen us, and Satan wants to destroy us. God and Satan will never have the same motivation. What Satan believes can destroy us, God enables us to bear. Know this: Whatever is allowed to come into your life has a limit.

In Genesis 50, we read that Joseph looked at his brothers after they had sold him into slavery and lied to his father, Jacob, about his whereabouts and said, "As for you, you meant evil against me, but God meant it for good in order to bring about this present result, to preserve many people alive" (Gen. 50:20). God's eternal perspective in Joseph's circumstance was to preserve many people alive. God allowed Joseph to undergo mind-crushing trials so that thousands would live. Satan might have wanted to destroy Joseph's significance, but Joseph was significant because he chose to champion his trials. Both Job's and Joseph's trials had a limit. God protected them from what would permanently crush them. Our Father does the same for us.

God Must Be Your Focus

God's sovereignty over everything is Christianity 101. But often it is a difficult attitude for us to acknowledge. Take a tip from our boy Job:

> Naked I came from my mother's womb, and naked I shall return there. The LORD gave and the LORD has taken away. Blessed be the name of the LORD (Job 1:21).

The moment you become aware of a trial in your life until the moment it ends, God must be your focus. He knows the way out of the difficulty and He will give you the wisdom to master it as you take it day by day; but you must seek Him.

> Fixing our eyes on Jesus, the author and perfecter of faith, who for the joy set before Him endured the cross, despising the shame, and has sat down at the right hand of the throne of God (Heb. 12:2).

Women, in general, have a strong desire to share their trials with whoever will listen. We tend to grab the phone immediately when we get hit with a crazy trial. We want comfort, answers and support. Little do we know that when we choose to seek the mere wisdom of other people without seeking God first, we pacify the desperate need we have for the Lord's direction. After talking to a friend, we then feel vindicated and heard, and sometimes we forget to even seek the Lord about it. This is a fatal mistake when surfing a trial.

A person will never have all the facts. But God does. It is vital to seek Him first before consulting any flesh. You don't want to make

God an afterthought; the same God that allowed the trial has the GPS for you to navigate out of it, and there is no better way out than the Lord when navigating a trial.

> But seek first His kingdom and His righteousness, and all these things will be added to you (Matt. 6:33).

When you have consulted God first, then and only then seek counsel from wise, Christian influences in your life. The words of these people will serve as confirmation of what the Lord has told you. For instance, you may be having financial issues. You have sought the Lord and God has told you to sell your car. When you meet with your wise counselors, they will more than likely confirm what God has already told you. Godly influences who have a relationship with God will counsel you with what God has told them. The counsel from God and a godly counselor will always match because God will tell the counselor the same thing He has told you. This is why when I make decisions for The Blush Network, I will normally pray about a decision and ask a few others to pray for a couple of days. When the days are complete, we will meet, and we always have the same resolution for the problem.

> Where there is no guidance the people fall, but in abundance of counselors there is victory (Prov. 11:14).

There have been a few times in my life when I had very little support on a couple of decisions. Even my wise counsel wasn't supportive. Sometimes God gets you to a point where He wants all voices to fade and for you to be obedient to Him alone. This type of decision is extremely hard. Stepping out alone in faith to do something that isn't really supported takes confirmation, not from friends, but from the Lord. In these types of circumstances, you must ask the Lord to confirm:

> In my distress I called upon the LORD, and cried to my God for help; He heard my voice out of His temple, and my cry for help before Him came into His ears (Ps. 18:6).

On one work trip, I was walking on the beach alone and praying. I had been having the most amazing time with the Lord. He was speaking so clearly to me about several things for the ministry and my future. I walked by a lady who was trying to take a picture of a beautiful tall bird that was walking in the waves. I felt the Lord tell me, *Go give her a hug.* I spoke right back to the Lord in my spirit, *Um, no way; she'll think I am crazy.*

I kept walking and heard the Lord speak to me again, *Go give her a hug.* This time, I was a little closer to her and struck up a short conversation with her and gave her a little pat on the back, thinking this would suffice for the affection the Lord wanted me to give her, and I walked on. After I took a few steps, the Lord said, *Go give her a hug.*

Finally, I told the Lord, *Okay, if she is still standing there when I turn around, I will give her a hug.* So when I turned around, sure enough, she was still trying to take a picture of that bird. I walked up to her, but not before looking up to the sky and in a firm voice saying, *A little help here, Lord. What do I say? Do I just walk up to her with my arms spread and give her a hug?* He responded, *Tell her whatever she is going through, she will be okay.*

When I got close to her, I asked if I could talk to her for a second. She said, "Sure." I said, "This may sound crazy, but I am a Christian, and as I was walking on the beach, God told me to tell you that whatever you are facing right now, you are going to be all right! God loves you so much, and He is going to take care of you."

When I was done speaking, I gave her that hug. Before I even pulled back from her, she was in tears. She said, "I can't believe you just said that. I am one of the government employees who got furloughed because of the shutdown, and I only have $200 to my name. I was just coming out here to pray and ask God what I am supposed to do."

We both stood there and cried. I was crying because I couldn't believe I was even resistant to what God clearly was asking me to do; and she was crying because she was completely relieved from the weight of her trial.

I didn't have a friend to ask about giving the lady a hug. I just continued to ask the Lord to confirm. His confirmation that day was louder in my spirit than in any phone conversation. I knew, without a doubt, that if I didn't obey, I would have been sinning. Thank God He gave me the grace, because that sweet woman received comfort from Him during her harsh trial.

Don't Fight the Trial; Fight the Temptation to Give Up Under It

> Through all this Job did not sin nor did he blame God (Job 1:22).

When a situation seems too much to bear, sometimes all you can think about is to give up. I have looked up to the sky and said, "Lord, I want to quit; help me out." The first place Satan will hit you when the trial gets out of hand is to cause you to want to give up. Discouragement and doubt set in almost immediately when you are faced with an insurmountable mountain. This subconscious testing serves as a major part of the trial itself.

Recovering alcoholics sometimes go back to drinking when a challenge gets too hard. People who are addicted to prescription drugs tend to run back to the arms of prescription comfort when circumstances overwhelm them. Allowing discouragement and doubt to stay in your thoughts will manifest in psychological torment that maximizes the weight of the trial. So you must watch your mind as much as your circumstances.

Stopping a thought when it first enters your mind is much easier to do than when you have meditated on it for a day or a week. The taunt of the trial is sometimes worse than the actual trial. Understand, sweet friend, that Satan desires to destroy your victorious thought patterns, especially when you are surfing a trial. If he can get you to believe even a little lie, he has won a piece of the victory that is yours. Let me reiterate: If you are a Christian, you hold the power to overcome. The day you want to give up the most is the day you need to dig your heels in.

Fighting a trial rather than facing it leads to a longer season of trial. For example, when Eddie and I got married, we lived way outside of our means. We could not afford to live the way we lived; however, I didn't want to live any less than we did. I really liked having new clothes and a nice house to live in. When faced with bills we couldn't pay, we began to rob Peter to pay Paul. Our finances were in disarray, and rather than deal with it, we would get another credit card. You can imagine the huge mess we ended up in!

Eventually, with a mortgage and a small baby, there came a time when we had to face the consequences. I fought it tooth and nail, but in the end, God clearly showed me that I was disobeying because I was not being a good steward of the money He had given us. So, we decided to face it. I started cleaning houses under the name "Maid in Heaven" and earned a little extra money. Eddie and I also started a paper route.

Now, understand, that was the last thing we wanted to do; however, fighting the reality that our money was out of control had only put us in more debt. Taking action against it got us out of debt. Every time we cut up a bill or credit card, we were victorious. We worked on it little by little, and God gave us victory.

Championing a Trial Positions You for Blessing

Once again, let's measure a godly attitude in the midst of trial by Job's words: "Though He slay me, I will hope in Him" (Job 13:15).

I dare say the blessings I find myself enjoying today have absolutely nothing to do with me. Faced with difficult trials for years, I have found that I have only had one option. I have learned that the only way is to live dependent on the Lord. Without Him, I would be addicted to some sort of substance or be a complete lunatic. I know that my mind and instinct fail every time under the goodness of my King. I am not under the illusion that I know everything like I was once thought. In fact, the longer I live, the more I realize that I know nothing apart from my Jesus Christ crucified. He is all I need to know. His acceptance is what I desire, and His presence bids me stand in the midst of the heaviest trials, because I have learned that if He has asked me to go through it, He has a reason for it.

We see God's hand all through the Old Testament with the children of Israel. When the Egyptians got scared that the growing nation of Israel would rise up against them in war and defeat them, the pharaoh decided, after consulting his people, to appoint taskmasters over the Israelites to afflict them with hard labor (see Exod. 1:11). But here's what happened:

> But the more they afflicted them, the more they were multiplied and the more they spread out, so that they were in dread of the sons of Israel (Exod. 1:12).

The harder the affliction the more they were blessed. The Israelites might not have been aware of it, but God was blessing the affliction. He is for His people, and no matter what the authorities did to God's people they were not the final authority. The final authority, God, turned that time of severe labor into a time of blessing. You may not see it now, sweet friend, but no one will have the last word like the Faithful and True. He is building your character, your legacy, your perseverance, your faith, your example to others and your ability to minister to them when they need you.

> The LORD restored the fortunes of Job when he prayed for his friends, and the LORD increased all that Job had twofold (Job 42:10).

Job felt the favor of the Lord that is assured to those who suffer and victoriously fight the fight of faith. Job's last days were increased twofold over the first part of his life. Job would not have benefited if he had given up. His determination unlocked the gifts that are only privy to us through the hand of the Lord.

My heart is with you, sweet warrior. There is no prize like living the call of God. Press on!

> I press on toward the goal for the prize of the upward call of God in Christ Jesus (Phil. 3:14).

QUESTIONS THAT SEEK TRUTH

1. Name a trial you are currently facing. What is one lesson you have learned?

2. When going through a trial, we are often tempted to believe that God is mad at us. Correction and trials are not the same thing. We go through trials to increase our faith. What trial have you mistaken for a correction?

3. In Job's life, God chose to remove Job's hedge of protection so that Satan could try him. Can you describe a time in your life when you felt that your hedge of protection was removed?

4. Fear is not fact; it is the impending thought of "What if?" When we factor God out of our trial, fear is a very real struggle. What fear or fears have you dealt with on a frequent basis?

5. Take comfort that God sets the limits for the trial. Just when we are ready to give up under the pressure of a trial is the time when we need to dig deeper and see God's hand. Has God ever ended one of your trials with a miracle? Explain.

6. If you give up, you continue in the trial. The only way to produce perseverance is to see the trial through. Where do you put your focus during your trials? How has your answer changed after reading this chapter?

7. "Through all of this Job did not sin nor did he blame God" (Job 1:22). It's easy to blame God when you go through a tough situation and can't see the outcome that He is producing wisdom in you. Think about a time when you blamed God for a hardship, not setting your eyes on the purpose behind it. What did you eventually learn? What will you do differently when your next trial comes?

8. The taunt of the trial is actually worse than the trial itself. Your thought patterns affect your navigation of the hardship. When have your thought patterns dictated your actions during a trial in negative ways? When have your thoughts affected your actions in positive ways?

9. "Though He slay me, I will hope in Him" (Job 13:15). At the end of Job's life, he was given a double blessing for the trials he successfully came through. When have you gone through a trial that turned into a blessing? Have you ever received a change of circumstances in the midst of a trial that resulted in more blessing than you could have imagined? Explain.

10. The more the Israelites were afflicted, the more they multiplied (see Exod. 1:12). What is your take on my words that the harder the trial, the greater the blessing? When has this been true in your life?

7

The Significance of Faith

I have never felt significant; I have huge insecurity issues.
Blush attendee

What would you change about your life if you were convinced faith was significant?

"God is too risky," I rationalized to excuse my lack of faith. My mindset was that if I couldn't control it, I wasn't going to do it. I felt safe in the realm of analysis. Making sense of my world brought me great comfort. If I could come up with a good enough reason for a decision, I would inevitably go with it.

Even though I was a believer, total trust in God felt like a risky proposition. After all, I had prayers that went unanswered; I had needs that weren't met to my liking; I had rejection baggage that followed me everywhere I went. The impossible seemed like a fairy-tale that I would never star in.

After I asked Jesus to save me, I did not seek to live by faith; therefore, increased faith did not become a part of my life. I was happy to just get saved from hell, and that's all I thought I needed. After all, my life was okay. It may not have been flashy, but it was all right. I was getting by. I was a good person. Those very lines, as I type them, are polarizing.

By the age of 22, living my way and not doing what God wanted me to do got me divorced and rejected from the very cushion of comfort I clung to.

When I finally chose to commit to a life of faith during the tragic years of my first marriage, the self-labeled "risky God" I had hidden from became the most tremendous haven I have ever found.

The Almighty God, Yahweh, the one and only God, is *not* risky. He does not ask us to do things that are out of line with His ultimate plan for our lives. I agree that faith is not easy, but refusing to follow the Lord in faith brings great loss to our lives. When God asks us to do something, and we falter in fear, we are missing something that will bring us great blessing. On the other hand, Christians who act on the urgings of the Holy Spirit, to follow His way, live in such a way that we all want what they have. And when we are privy to the same blessings, we realize it is because we have utilized the power of faith.

Satan wants us to believe that God is too risky to get close to and His ways are tricky and reckless. That's because He knows that faith in God is the quickest way to blessing.

> And without faith it is impossible to please Him, for he who comes to God must believe that He is and that He is a rewarder of those who seek Him (Heb. 11:6).

Without faith, you have absolutely no chance of pleasing God. You cannot please Him unless you listen and obey. Obedience plays a huge part in faith. We teach our children to obey when we ask them to do something that, to them, may sound crazy. The same applies to God. Obeying His request of you, by faith, is necessary to be in right standing with Him.

A life of faith means that we believe that God is who He says He is, and we trust Him to be all that He says He is and all that He says He will do. This is tricky for us to understand, so let me say it plainly. Romans 10:17 says, "Faith comes by hearing, and hearing by the word of Christ" (*NKJV*). Faith and hope are two totally different things. You cannot have faith unless you have a promise or assurance (see Heb. 11:1). If we have a promise given by God from His Word, we can believe that promise will happen. Without confirmation from God's Word of a promise, you cannot have expectation. You cannot have faith in something that is not promised. For instance, God promised me a traveling conference ministry; I had faith that it would happen because He confirmed it through His word in Habakkuk 2:2-4. I have the assurance of things not seen. When you have a desire you believe God has placed in your heart, go to your Bible for confirmation. If God gives you a verse through His Word, stand on that promise until it comes to pass. Otherwise you will waste your time struggling with the doubt that will surely come. When you have His confirmation, you can expect the thing to come to pass.

When trials come, do you believe that God will take care of your needs? No matter what your flesh tells you, God is who His Word says He is. There is not one untruth in the Bible. When you begin to believe that He is who He says He is, His charge to be a person of faith gets easier.

Faith and blessing are buddies. I tell you the truth, I have never stepped out in faith and not been blessed. Every time I do what God tells me to do, I am overcome by the blessing of His rewards. You cannot make a step of faith that God doesn't bless. A decision to move forward with something God has told me to do, no matter the risk, always proves to be right, even if, in the moment, what God has asked me to do seems crazy. The Lord has never led me astray or put me to shame. He has never embarrassed me. Quite the opposite; following Him has given me things I could never have achieved without stepping out in faith. I have concluded that if God is asking, I must follow, believing. I have no other choice.

Now that I think of it, every time God has asked me to do something, it has never made logical sense according to my finite mind. Why? His ways are so much higher than mine.

"For My thoughts are not your thoughts, nor are your ways My ways," declares the Lord. "For as the heavens are higher than the earth, so are My ways higher than your ways and My thoughts than your thoughts" (Isa. 55:8-9).

God wants you to experience the riches of His glory. He wants you to go higher than you ever thought possible and achieve more than you ever thought you could. When God authored your life, He saw the maximum blessing you could receive. He painted your life as fruitful; now He is waiting on you to believe and trust Him in order to shower you with the blessings your faith engages. He is your Father who desperately wants great things for His child.

You are the deciding factor. You have the option to be disobedient in the area of faith; but let me warn you, amazing blessings with your name written on them will never be showered on you if you choose to disobey. When you forgo the opportunity to champion God's will for your life, you do not know what you are saying no to. Your significant calling will never be achieved without faith.

Beginning Steps of The Blush Network

Faith is not easy. Some of the hardest moments of my life have been moments when I chose faith. I am living now in the blessing of moving forward in that faith. If you want blessing and significance, you'll find it on the narrow trail called trust in God.

I remember sitting alone at a coffee shop a couple of years after we had moved to Indiana so that Eddie could be a youth pastor at a church there. As I was sipping my coffee that morning, I felt the Lord speak to my spirit and say, "Get ready." In those few words impressed upon my spirit, I knew that God was getting ready to change the course of our lives. I had felt for some time that our time at this particular church was limited. I knew that God wanted to take us in a different direction, but He wanted us to follow His leading and obey as He spoke. I went home and didn't tell Eddie of the impression that day, but just a couple of days later, Eddie walked in the door and said, "I think it's time for us to move on." When he spoke, I knew that God was moving us to a new assignment.

At that time, we had a baby, no money, a mortgage and no promise of another job. So we began to pray. Before Eddie gave his notice, we attempted to find him another position due to the pressure of our financial needs. God, however, wanted our faith and complete obedience, so we found nothing.

One of the executive pastors at the church had set up a dinner meeting with us. As we sat there, we knew what God wanted us to do, and before much conversation began, Eddie said, "It's time for us to move on." I'm not sure what Eddie's boss thought, but in that moment, peace poured over me—God's inexplicable peace that is one of the greatest blessings I have ever known. We awkwardly finished dinner and walked out in full confidence that we had done exactly what God wanted us to do.

The next day, everything hit the fan as our dearest friends started calling and asking us why we were moving on. Our answer was simple: "God told us to." One person even told Eddie that this decision wasn't God's will. Looking back at the situation, I can almost understand their concern; we had no money, and we had a mortgage and a baby. However, we were confident in the call. We moved forward unwaveringly with the unpopular decision to do exactly what God wanted us to do.

To our complete excitement, our house sold in three weeks. The market was dead in Indiana, so it was a miracle that our house sold. When we sat at the closing of our house with the buyers, and they asked us, "Where are you moving to?" our answer surprised them when we said, "We have no idea."

One man looked at Eddie and said, "Do you think you are going to get a job better than *this*?" Eddie's reply was that it didn't matter; God had told us to move. About a month later, God blessed Eddie with a job that he could only have dreamed about, and we moved to Phoenix, Arizona. Because of our move to Phoenix, and several circumstances there, God positioned us to be at a place to found The Blush Network. If we hadn't moved when we did, we would have missed God's blessings for us.

This move was difficult, and I clung to the verse in Hebrews 11:8, which says, "By faith, Abraham, when he was called, obeyed by going out to a place which he was to receive for an inheritance; and he went out, not knowing where he was going."

After we saw God blow our minds and reward our faith, it gave us greater faith. That was our first large test as a married couple. God had simply bid us obey, and it was up to us to answer the call.

A Pattern for Faith in Action

The very first act of faith recorded in the Bible is the faith of Noah. You may know the story; its details are a blueprint of the way God calls us to a faithful act. In Genesis 6, we read of God's relationship with Noah. We see that the Lord saw man and that "every intent of the thoughts of his heart was only evil continually" (Gen. 6:5).

God was sorry He had made man, so He decided to blot out man from the face of the earth. But Noah found favor in His sight (see vv. 6-8). Noah must have been a righteous man, because God decided to save his life.

God Spoke to Noah and Gave Him a Reason

> Then God said to Noah, "The end of all flesh has come before Me; for the earth is filled with violence because of them; and behold, I am about to destroy them with the earth" (Gen. 6:13).

Before God even told Noah the act of faith He wanted Noah to follow, He gave Noah the problem, the reason for it. He wanted Noah to know that what He was getting ready to ask Noah to do would be crazy except for the fact that He was getting ready to destroy all living things on the earth.

God always gives us a reason before He asks us to move. In Indiana, I knew exactly why God wanted us to move; God had been very clear to both Eddie and me that He wanted something better for us. His plan for our lives in that place was completed. He told us that long before "the ask" happened.

God Instructed Noah with a Charge

> Make for yourself an ark of gopher wood; you shall make the ark with rooms, and shall cover it inside and out with pitch (Gen. 6:14).

God gave Noah a clear directive and asked him to make the ark. Now, this was crazy! It had never even rained on earth up to this time. However, faith never makes logical sense until it is realized. The same thing happened with Eddie and me when we moved. God told both of us that the time was at hand.

God Directed Noah with an Action Step

> This is how you shall make it: the length of the ark three hundred cubits, its breadth fifty cubits, and its height thirty

cubits. You shall make a window for the ark, and finish it to
a cubit from the top; and set the door of the ark in the side
of it; you shall make it with lower, second and third decks
(Gen. 6:15-16).

God was very specific with Noah about how to build the ark, because
there were a ton of animals that needed to go into that ark that
wouldn't have fit otherwise. When God calls you to faith, He has a
detailed plan that He rolls out before you. God is a God of order,
not chaos, and He wants His direction to be followed to ensure that
you are confident in His leadership. In the same way, God wanted
Eddie and me to take a step of faith and quit the job Eddie had so
that he could have time to search for another one. God knew that if
we didn't sell our house when we did, we would have missed part of
His blessing. His direction was that clear.

God Reaffirmed the Plan to Noah

Behold, I, even I am bringing the flood of water upon the earth,
to destroy all flesh in which is the breath of life, from under
heaven; everything that is on the earth shall perish (Gen. 6:17).

In the midst of blind faith, we often start to freak out. We see that we
are in the middle of doing something that we know God wants us to
do, but we start looking at our circumstances and say to ourselves,
Did I hear God right? Am I crazy? What we are doing doesn't seem to
make any sense to us, and then God, in His loving way, will swoop
down and repeat Himself. He reaffirms that we are not crazy.

I have felt crazy so many times when I have stepped out in faith,
but God always answers my weak moments with overwhelming acts
of confirmation. He loves you; and all along the faith process, He will
remind you that you are on the right track.

God Promised Noah a Reward

But I will establish My covenant with you; and you shall enter
the ark—you and your sons and your wife, and your sons' wives
with you (Gen. 6:18).

In the threat of impending destruction, God saved Noah and his family. Imagine the stages of shock Noah went through hearing from the Lord, maybe for the first time, and the first thing God said was, "I'm going to kill everyone with water." That is enough to make anyone feel crazy! But God promised Noah blessing, reward and his life.

You will not act on faith and then go unrewarded. It is against God's way. He is pleased with every act that He knows is counter to the flesh and takes courage to do. The reward may not come when you want it or how you want it; but hear me now: it *will* come.

Noah's Response to God's Plan

> Thus Noah did; according to all that God had commanded him, so he did (Gen. 6:22).

We, of course, know the rest of the story. Noah, his wife and their three sons—Shem, Ham and Japheth—and their wives populated the whole earth.

What if Noah had laughed off God's instruction and had not built the ark? The entire human race would have ceased. I wouldn't be sitting here on a chair, looking at the ocean, if Noah had said, "No, I won't do it; that's crazy." His blind obedience and resolute decision to take God at His word paid off.

How to Be Like Noah

Living a life of faith will be the most challenging, tumultuous, overwhelming thing you have ever done; and in the midst of it you will face opposition.

Silence the Naysayers

> "Let God be true but every man a liar" is the language of true faith.—A. W. Tozer

Satan does not want you to exhibit faith, because a life of faith is contagious. People will see what you are doing and want the same blessing that you have. When they find out you are simply following the Lord, it catches on.

Some people, however, will try to discourage you. When the man said to Eddie, "Moving isn't God's will for your life," it was one of the most hurtful, discouraging things he could have said, and he was wrong. There will be people who do not understand your leap of faith, and that is okay. Let them be puzzled; in the end, God will shut their mouths. You don't even have to explain! God will do the explaining. He is your Advocate!

I'm sure that everyone and their moms told Noah he was a nut job; but they are dead now, and not from natural causes after a long life! Eventually, God silenced all the naysayers. When God says it, you need to do it. You will never win the positive opinion of some people, and if you try, it will exhaust you. Silence the naysayers in your mind and let the Lord speak.

Let Fear Give Way to Faith

> Be watchful, stand firm in the faith, act like men, be strong
> (1 Cor. 16:13, *ESV*).

Fear and faith are not friends. There have been times on my faith journey when I have awakened in the middle of the night in a panic about what I am doing. Onslaughts of fear are the enemy's way of scaring you out of God's plan. He wants to paralyze you and keep you from doing what God wants, because he knows you will further God's kingdom if he doesn't keep you fearful. An onslaught of fear is extra strong after you have quit a job, moved across the country, bought a house, and so on. Don't give in to the fear! Hold up your shield of faith (see Eph. 6:16) and block the enemy.

When I am struck with debilitating fear, I hit the floor on my knees. Prayer is the most effective artillery against such fierce fear.

You Are Never Alone

You may look around after you step out in faith and think that you are standing alone. You can rest in the knowledge that you have engaged the power of Almighty God. The great I AM stands with you. His regard for you is great, and His sovereign power will aid your faith stance. The times when I have felt the loneliest after a huge decision to move forward in faith, God has always reminded me that He is right by my side.

Faith Is Counter to the Flesh

[Jesus spoke to His disciples and said], "Why are you afraid, you men of little faith?" Then he got up and rebuked the winds and the sea, and it became perfectly calm (Matt. 8:26).

Walking by faith and not by sight is something you can do only when you are walking in the Spirit of God. Our flesh doesn't agree with acts of faith. It can't understand it. When we are trying to do great acts of faith for the Lord and we haven't had our time in the Word and in prayer, we will not follow through on those acts. We must be fed, on a regular basis, by the Word of God and spend focused time with Him in order to even attempt what God has for us.

Time with God is a must when facing giant leaps of faith. You may desire to be great for God, but are you ready to put in the work by getting to know God in order to do what He asks?

When Faith Becomes Sight, Your Faith Grows

[Jesus] said to them, "Because of the littleness of your faith. For truly I say to you, if you have faith the size of a mustard seed, you will say to this mountain, 'Move from here to there,' and it will move; and nothing will be impossible to you" (Matt. 17:20).

When God first told me to start a traveling young-women's conference ministry, it sounded crazy to me. *What, God? Me?* was my response. But after 10 years and huge miracles, I have seen God honor that step of faith over and over again. Every time I see another blessing because of the small amount of faith it took to begin The Blush Network, I am reminded of the incredibly great God

I serve. My faith continues to grow because my God never fails. Triumphing through living a life of faith is the only way to live.

Several years ago, I wrote in my Bible the words "By Faith, Autumn" at the beginning of Hebrews 11, which is called the faith chapter. It's a good reminder to me on days when my faith falters a bit. I don't want to live a boring Christian life, because my God is not boring.

Champion your life for God! May your life be defined and characterized by your courageous walk of faith.

QUESTIONS THAT SEEK TRUTH

1. I used to think that walking by faith was too risky. I didn't trust the end result and thought it would end in my shame. When have you had these kinds of thoughts? Think of a couple of specific examples.

2. Without faith it is impossible to please God (see Heb. 11:6). When did you last step out in faith because you felt that was what God wanted you to do? What happened?

3. Faith and blessing are buddies. The blessed life is a life that trusts God through faith. Have you ever had a season of blessing that was a result of your faith? What would you tell others about that time?

4. The very first act of faith recorded in Scripture is the story of Noah and the ark (see Gen. 6–9). Noah was asked to build an ark and then God gave him the reason for it. When God requires acts of faith from you, He will give you a reason why. What story can you describe of a time when God gave you direction and a reason for it?

5. Noah was given a charge from God and he was then given all the details. Your act of faith will also have a clearly de-tailed charge. Have you been given a charge right now that you are hesitating to do?

6. After giving Noah direction, God reaffirmed His reasons. When we question what God is asking us to do, He always reaffirms the reason through prayer, the Bible, or through the counsel of a godly individual. When have you experienced a time that God answered your insecurity about an act of faith with a confirmation?

7. Do you feel like you will be rewarded for your faith? Why or why not?

8. Has there ever been a time when God specifically told you to do something and everyone around you disagreed that it was God speaking? Explain.

9. Because acts of faith are outside of our control, fear has the tendency to overwhelm us before and after we step out. What is one way you can fight fear when you believe that God is asking you to do something?

10. Although you may feel alone when you are stepping out in faith, the power of God goes with you. When have you felt the presence of God with you when you stepped out in faith?

8

The Significance of the Wait

Sometimes I go through life just existing. In those times, I'm never satisfied. I am only productive in my thoughts and actions when I am purpose driven. To be honest, I'm struggling between the two right now.

BLUSH ATTENDEE

What is the difference between just existing and waiting in faith?

Grrrrrr! I hate to wait! I'm the girl in the line at the coffee shop who always gets stuck behind the person who orders the triple shot–extra hot decaf–two pumps of caramel–no foam person. Yep, that's me behind you, tapping my foot because it is taking you forever to order.

I even record all of my TV shows and watch them with no commercials because I don't like waiting through commercials. Yep, I hate to wait. But God in His love has often forced me to.

Waiting is one of the most difficult disciplines God has us experience. It has a way of teaching us the deep mysteries of God without anything seeming to happen. Waiting plays on every insecurity we have; it rattles us to the core. When God asks us to wait, it can feel like the emotional equivalent of clicking up to the top of a roller-coaster ride and sitting there for a while before the start of the plunge. Some days we feel like a warrior, completely confident in what we are waiting for; there are other days when we whine and cry because the wait seems so cruel. Everyone, at some point, is asked to wait—it is inevitable.

The significant thing about waiting is the power and audacity it can produce. Waiting does not discriminate on whom it descends, and it will not disappoint when the thing waited for materializes.

I sat in a beautifully ornate chair outside the host house in which I was living. I had divorced my abusive husband the previous year and was chosen as a female intern by Liberty University to serve at a church in Columbus, Ohio. I acted as the girl leader for the youth group. It was such a great time for me. I remember going to work every day with a sense of purpose that my future was extremely bright. I had learned to accept the fact that I was a 23-year-old divorcée. I knew that God had brought me out of a horrific time in my life, and I knew that He was not even close to done with me.

For two years, I had been asking God what He wanted to do with me. I wanted my direction to be clear so that I would not veer from the path He had chosen for me. I prayed earnestly for direction. I knew my gifts; I loved to do public speaking—my soul thrilled to share passionately with others about what God can do with a life that has been surrendered to His hand. I knew that I had some leadership gifts, because I had always been a personality that liked to take charge in any situation. People looked to me for direction. The Lord allowed me to remember my gifts even though they had been hidden for years.

I had developed a small interest in conference ministry even though I didn't know anything about it. I definitely didn't feel qualified to *lead* a conference ministry, because I had some major skeletons in my closet the church didn't seem to accept. Divorced at age 22 seemed to disqualify me to do just about anything in ministry. But I knew that God was working in my heart.

That hot day in June, as I sat outside, my chair seemed to be like a throne that God used to speak to me. I was busy studying Ephesians 6 to get ready to speak on the armor of God. I relished every fresh point God was teaching me. Then I stopped reading, and I began to pray, desperately asking God to show me what He wanted to do with my life. I begged God to be clear. As I opened my eyes from intense prayer, I looked at my beloved blue Bible and saw that it was open to Habakkuk 2:1-3—a passage I had never seen before. I began to read, and every word I read seemed to speak directly to me. I read fast to see what the whole passage had to say. Habakkuk, the minor prophet, spoke these words:

> I will stand on my guard post and station myself on the rampart; and I will keep watch to see what He will speak to me, and how I may reply when I am reproved. Then the LORD answered and said, "Record the vision and inscribe it on tablets, that the one who reads it may run. For the vision is yet for the appointed time; it hastens toward the goal and it will not fail. Though it tarries, wait for it; for it will certainly come, it will not delay."

I sat speechless as I let that passage of Scripture sink in to my broken, desperate, healing heart. God had spoken to me so directly about my future that it was unmistakable. He had asked me to start a conference ministry, and I was happy to accept that call on my life. He was clear about it. The moment was so powerful that I will never forget it.

Along with the call on my life came the call to wait. He had been gracious to me because He told me right then, "Though it tarries, wait for it." So I began my wait. Year after year, I waited and prayed with no sign of the promise's fulfillment. There were days when I would be so encouraged by God's Word that I felt like I could wait forever. There were other days when I felt like a fool waiting for something that looked like it would never happen.

Satan told me over and over that I was nobody, and who would listen to a washed-up, messed-up "Christian" like me? Some days I gave in to those lies and found myself battling a pit of despair. But I never forgot what God had told me. The words "though it tarries, wait for it" circulated in my mind. The Holy Spirit reminded me that God couldn't lie, because it is against His very nature. Remembering this gave me the stamina I needed to wait just a little longer. God would encourage me when the frustration swelled. And I waited.

Ten years passed since I began praying for God to use my hurts. Though the wait seemed long, I had somehow grown comfortable with it. Then my waiting ended. Eddie came home early from work one day and told me that he had been laid off for financial reasons. I knew when I heard the garage door open at 11:00 A.M. that morning something was terribly wrong. The look on Eddie's face was all I needed to know. But then a sense of assurance fell over me rather than fear. I felt the Holy Spirit say very strongly to my spirit: "It's going to be okay."

Eddie interviewed with many different churches for another youth pastor position. The interview process was different from any other we had ever done, namely because I knew without a doubt that God was getting ready to launch the conference ministry for which I had prayed for so many years. Eddie was offered a job in Dallas, but we hadn't met the pastor of the church yet, which was imperative, because we would be joining the staff to further the pastor's vision for the church, and we needed to make sure we were able to support him.

We flew to Dallas just to meet him. I entered the pastor's office and I remember looking at the Dallas skyline when my eyes wandered to the wall of books he had written; there were 19 books, to be exact. The sight was intimidating. We talked a little bit after we sat down, but I had a very important question for him and waited for my turn to ask it. The pastor was gracious and kind as he told us of his excitement at having us on staff. The moment came when he turned to me and asked me how I was feeling. I remember thinking, *This is my moment*. I told him as confidently as I could that I knew why he would want Eddie to be on his team, but I believed very strongly that Eddie was not the only one with a calling on his life. I talked about the young women's conference calling.

He let me finish, and then he said that he believed in me and would support me in beginning the conference at the church. You can imagine the emotions that came over me. I was so overwhelmed by his words that I began to cry. I believed those words would be spoken to me one day—and the moment they were spoken, my faith grew exponentially, because it solidified the call on my life. It was a transforming moment. It marked the materialization of the beginning of the ministry God allowed me to found: The Blush Network. The wait had finally ended.

Let's Get Real

I wonder what you are waiting for today. It could be anything from having children to getting a promotion at work. Waiting is necessary for the realization of anything great. If you take a stroll through Scripture, you will see that the most amazing things took time.

Beginning with Genesis 1, the earth took seven days to create. Could God have created the world in one second? *Absolutely*. However, by His design, He chose to draw out the process for seven days. Look at Noah—God told him to build the ark and gather two of every animal, then the rain came and lasted for 40 days. Could God have wiped the earth clear of every living thing in a second? *Absolutely*. However, He wanted to use the principle of time to fulfill His will.

Think of Moses—how annoying do you think it was for him to go to Pharaoh and ask him to let the Israelites go? God could have allowed Pharaoh to say yes the first time Moses asked, but God's will defined the time frame. Time and consequence wore Pharaoh down until the time came to produce immense glory for the Lord.

How about the wait to enter to the Promised Land? As a result of their lack of faith and disobedience, God had Moses lead the Israelites in the wilderness for 40 years before they were ready to enter.

King David was anointed king years before he actually took the throne when he was 30. When Jesus died on the cross, God's design was that He would be in the grave for three days before He rose from the dead.

Unfortunate but Needed Delays

You are in good company if you are waiting for something. I know what it feels like. But I want you to look at some reasons from Scripture that may be lengthening your wait:

> Therefore, the LORD longs to be gracious to you, and therefore He waits on high to have compassion on you. For the Lord is a God of justice; How blessed are all those who long for Him (Isa. 30:18).

I love to cross-reference. So let's look at Isaiah 42:14:

> I have kept silent for a long time; I have kept still and restrained Myself. Now like a woman in labor I will groan, I will both grasp and pant.

The Lord is not slow about His promise, as some count slowness, but is patient toward you, not wishing for any to perish but for all to come to repentance (2 Pet. 3:9).

All three passages of Scripture talk about the Lord waiting on us. In Isaiah 30:18 in my study, I was intrigued by the word "therefore." So I looked much deeper into this passage. Looking up just a few verses to find out why God uses "therefore," I found the reason in verse 15:

For thus the Lord GOD, the Holy One of Israel, has said, "In repentance and rest you will be saved, in quietness and trust is your strength." But you were not willing (Isa. 30:15).

Now, the Lord God, the Holy One of Israel, is interpreted to mean Yahweh. It is the supreme use of the term "Lord." The Lord, the supreme God, is speaking here. So it's time for us to take notice of what He says. This passage of Scripture is talking about the nation of Israel. This is the nation that was God's chosen people. This is the bloodline that fought and was successful in defeating the great giants of old; and God delivered them from Egypt via the parting of the Red Sea. This was the nation that had seen miracles. However, when they reached the Promised Land, they began to forget. They began to worship pagan gods and marry people from other nations that were off limits to them. They made alliances that God didn't approve of and they executed plans that were not of the Lord's. Even when God warned them through prophets about changing their ways, they wouldn't change.

God was longing to be gracious to them; He was waiting on high to have compassion on them (see Isa. 30:18). God was longing for them to do what He said so that He could be gracious to them, but they were not willing. Isaiah 30:15 tells us that despite all that God had done for them and was waiting to do, they were not willing.

People are waiting for all sorts of things: spouses to get saved, children to get off drugs, freedom from addictions, employment—these are just a few things people wait for. In doing a ton of work among young women, I hear all the time, "I am waiting for a man." We are all waiting for something.

I know that I have waited. I have had my face to the ground, crying out to the Lord to come through because if He didn't come through I didn't know what I was going to do. But let me tell you, there are four things that God showed me that will ensure the end of your waiting.

> In repentance and rest you will be saved, in quietness and trust is your strength (Isa. 30:15).

Some of us, sweet reader, are waiting because we are not willing to do what God has asked of us. What does He ask of us? To *repent, rest, be quiet* and *trust*.

Repent. This is a tough one; I didn't want to put this one first, but it is the first one that God puts in the verse. Perhaps you need to have a good old-fashioned repentance session. You are waiting because there is sin that God literally cannot bless. You may know that. Whatever it is, if you don't know, ask God to reveal it to you. Deep down, you know what you are involved in that God cannot condone—sex, lies, gossip. Whatever it is, God cannot be gracious to someone who has built up a wall of sin until you repent of it. The first thing you need to do is repent.

Rest. My husband has no problem resting. He can fall asleep anywhere; but that is so hard for me. If you are reading this and saying, "I have repented over and over," your problem may be that you have not moved on to rest. Resting in the Lord is what you need to do. Your spirit is full of anxiety and does not allow you to rest. You may be so busy trying to make things happen that you have too much unrest in your spirit, which is causing you to wait longer. "Be still, and know that I am God" (Ps. 46:10, *ESV*).

Be quiet. Be quiet or at peace. After you have repented and rested, it's time to be at peace, believing the thing will happen when God wills it.

Trust. Trust is easy when it is the little things. I can trust in the small things, but trusting in the bigger things is difficult. It's easy to trust when we can control what we are trusting. God says, *Autumn, I have placed that dream outside of your reach so that you can learn to trust*

Me. I have made it outside the realm of your control so that you will trust Me to do the thing. He says, *I am longing to be gracious to you; I am longing to pour out My blessing on you; but I will not fulfill it if you have your hand wrapped around it and do not trust Me in it.* Let it go, sweet reader. Trust Him.

Your mouth has to match your actions. We may say that we are willing to do these things, but it is an act of complete obedience. Are you willing to repent? Are you willing to rest in Him? Are you willing to peacefully accept and be quiet while you wait? Are you willing to trust Him with the hard areas?

If You Are Willing, Here Is the Promise

These are the things He promises:

> You will weep no longer.
> He will surely be gracious to you at the sound of your cry;
> When He hears it, He will answer you;
> He will no longer hide Himself;
> He will give you a word, "This is the way; walk in it."
> He will give you rain for the seed you have sown in the ground;
> He will give you rich and plenteous bread;
> Your livestock will graze in a roomy pasture;
> There will be streams running with water;
> The light of the moon will be as the light of the sun;
> He will bind up the fracture of His people;
> He will heal the bruise He has afflicted (see Isaiah 30:19-26).

The mystery of the Lord is wrapped up in His Word. He may be waiting on you to do one of the four commands so that He can fulfill exactly what you are waiting for. Exercising those commands will ensure that blessing will come. He desperately longs to be gracious to you; He may simply be waiting on high for you.

The Importance of the Wait

> I wait for the LORD, my soul does wait, and in His word I do hope (Ps. 130:5).

Take encouragement from someone who has gone through the trial of the wait, sweet friend—it is for a very important reason. I thought God was almost cruel at times to have me continue waiting; but now, as president of The Blush Network, I can see that I was in no way ready to lead an organization in the early days of the wait. I thought I was ready so many times, but God in His beautiful sovereignty knew that I was far from it. Looking back, I am so grateful for the lesson of the wait. God brilliantly designed the wait to strengthen me spiritually, emotionally and mentally for what He knew was going to come with the responsibility.

The Importance of Enduring Victoriously

> I am weary with my crying; my throat is parched; my
> eyes fail while I wait for my God (Ps. 69:3).

My dear friend, take advantage of the process of the wait. There will be a time that the waiting period will be over. There will be no more wait. Are you going to be ready for the task when it presents itself? Are you taking full advantage of the waiting period that God has given you? Use this time to better prepare and strengthen yourself for when the wait ends rather than focusing on being frustrated about waiting for something.

I love this point when I talk with single girls. I know it is so difficult to wait for a long period of time for a mate. As women, we are designed to care for a man and to have him love us. My challenge to girls who are waiting and getting frustrated is to take advantage of the wait. Take it from me: Once you are married, you will never experience life the same way again. You will not be able to do all the things that you can do when you are single. Take advantage of your season of singleness. Don't complain about exactly where God has you; get busy finding out what you can do to please Him during this single period. Complaints, my beauty, don't please God. One of my favorite sayings is, "When opportunity knocks, it's too late to prepare." You must fully embrace the wait in order to enjoy the fulfilled promise.

The Importance of Education During the Wait

> Let integrity and uprightness preserve me, for I wait for
> You (Ps. 25:21).

There is wealth in the wait. There are lessons to learn while wait-ing that you can learn in no other circumstance. While you are in a place of waiting, seek God on what those lessons are. One of the things God taught me was to stand alone, with Him. Leading anything means you have to stand alone, at times, although people who love me surround me.

I learned to stand alone when I began to tell people of the call on my life. People looked at me as if I were crazy. I had to stand on the promise of what God had told me and force myself to believe what He had said rather than to please the person standing in front of me. My dependence on God grew as I saw others not as thrilled as I was about the idea of a conference ministry. There have been so many times while leading The Blush Network when I've known that the answer to a problem or issue came from God alone. God has grown my dependence on the divine and not the human.

The Importance of Waiting Expectantly

> But as for me, I will watch expectantly for the LORD; I will
> wait for the God of my salvation. My God will hear me
> (Mic. 7:7).

Sometimes the most amazing thing you can learn from a waiting period is faith. God says so clearly in the Bible that without faith, it is impossible to please God. Waiting and hoping for something, then seeing God come through, can only develop faith. It can re-quire a reckless abandonment of human logic, program or plan. It means counting on divine intervention to break the human logic and circumstance.

In Hebrews 11, we read of the amazing things that were accom-plished because people who were like you and me had the faith and common sense to take God at His word. They believed God, and it was counted to them as righteousness. I don't know about you, but my utmost desire is to be counted by God as a righteous woman. I desire for God to look at me one day in heaven and say, *Well done, Autumn.* I know that I must exude faith to please God, and if waiting is what it takes to develop that trait, then waiting is what must happen.

The Assurance of God's Presence During the Wait

> For He Himself has said, "I will never leave you nor forsake you" (Heb. 13:5, *NKJV*).

When you have had a rough day waiting for the thing that you have been promised, sometimes you assume that God has left you alone. His Word says, "I will never leave you nor forsake you." Do you believe this applies to you today? If you do, you can count on the fact that God waits with you every second of the waiting process. He feels the pain you struggle with in your darkest hour and He hears your cries when you just feel like you can't go on. He hurts with you. Yet, He loves you enough not to throw you into a situation prematurely. The last thing you want is to be put in a situation that you are unprepared for emotionally and spiritually. His love bids you wait until the timing is right and the circumstances are perfect.

The Certainty of His Promises

> For from days of old they have not heard or perceived by ear, nor has the eye seen a God besides You, Who acts on behalf of the one who waits for Him (Isa. 64:4).

One of the things that encourage me greatly in the Habakkuk passage of Scripture is that when God gives you a promise, He cannot fail to follow through, because that would be contrary to who He is. If He has promised you through His Word that you will have a baby, as He did with Abraham and Sarah, your responsibility is to believe Him. The problem with believers today is that they give up on the promises of God after a couple of months. We get discouraged and lose faith. I challenge you today to keep the faith.

Some of the apostle Paul's last words were, "I have fought the fight, I have finished the race, I have kept the faith" (2 Tim. 4:7). Was Paul's life easy? No. But he recognized that to live with Christ and exude faith was far better than to live a life without Him. Christ propelled Paul to keep the faith. When you lose heart after having received a direct promise, the only one who misses out is you. No one else is missing out when you opt out of believing what God has promised you, and you are in danger of losing a huge piece of your significance. Take it from someone who knows—it will blow your mind.

There Is No Time Lost When God Asks Us to Wait

I know that you may think that time is running out on your life. You feel that you are missing out because God has not come through in the time period you feel is favorable. Time may seem to be ticking, and you may even believe that your biological clock is ticking, but it isn't if it's not time.

God is aware of exactly the correct time to give you a child or a spouse. You are not losing time, dear reader; the time has not yet come. Don't get tripped up into thinking that your life is wasting away because the thing you are waiting for has not happened. Rest your mind from those thoughts and understand that if the time hasn't come for whatever you are waiting for, focus on where you are and what God wants to do with you where you are. He knows, sweet reader; He has not forgotten.

I want to tear apart the Habakkuk passage to encourage you on your journey of the wait:

I will stand on my guard post
And station myself on the rampart;
And I will keep watch to see what He will speak to me,
And how I may reply when I am reproved.
Then the LORD answered me and said,
"Record the vision
And inscribe it on tablets,
That the one who reads it may run.
"For the vision is yet for the appointed time;

It hastens toward the goal and it will not fail.
Though it tarries, wait for it;
For it will certainly come, it will not delay.
"Behold, as for the proud one,
His soul is not right within him;
But the righteous will live by his faith" (Hab. 2:1-4).

This passage gives us insight about Habakkuk's mental state and his level of expectancy. Look at the action he was taking in order to hear from God:

Stand on my guard post
Station myself on the rampart
Keep watch to see what He will speak to me.

Habakkuk was intentional about getting direction. He was so intentional that he literally poised himself mentally and emotionally to receive the answer to what he needed. It is our responsibility to position ourselves in a place to hear what God will say to us.

We get so incredibly busy that the thought of actually standing, stationing and watching never enters our mind. God is pleased when we expect Him to act. Habakkuk had an attitude of expectation; he knew that it was only a matter of time before God was going to say something, and he wanted to hear it badly enough that he stopped everything and waited. The amount of time it would take didn't faze him, and frustration was not an issue. He was intent on hearing from the Lord when the Lord showed up.

If you want to get serious about the direction of your life, three key elements are noted in the text.

Stand on Your Guard Post

Assume the position of authority. The action of standing on the guard post tells us that Habakkuk did not take this matter lightly. He did not sit or lie down. His position communicated a humble yet intentional call for guidance. Stand as if your life depended on it, because the abundant life God promises you does depend on it. The moment you decide to stop running in every direction to find significance and seek the only one worthy of giving you the very thing you want, something spiritual happens. Habakkuk acted as a guard. He positioned himself so that he wouldn't miss the message when God answered.

Station Yourself on the Rampart

Habakkuk was firmly planted on the rampart. A rampart is a geographical high place or a place that can be used as defense. A rampart is a place of visibility, which gave Habakkuk access to be the first informed. He stood stationary on his guard post located on the rampart. The stillness of his body made it hard to get distracted, which enabled him to be aware of God's voice when it came. Habakkuk's purpose was clear by his posture alone. This guy wasn't going anywhere.

Keep Watch for God's Answer

The action of keeping watch tells us that Habakkuk waited. The passage doesn't say when He will speak; it says "what" He will speak. Habakkuk knew that God was going to say something. He was so confident of God's presence that he watched vigilantly. He knew the answer was at hand.

And then heaven's gates were opened as if Habakkuk held the key to unlock them, and the Lord Almighty answered him. God's response gave Habakkuk action. These were the three action steps: (1) record the vision, (2) write it plainly on tablets, and (3) wait for God to give the message.

Record the Vision

God clearly provided a vision for Habakkuk, and his responsibility was to write it down. It was to be taken so seriously that it needed to be recorded in stone. It was absolute. God's vision for your life is no different. God has given each of us a significant calling on our lives, and the vision for it is so specific that it should be written down. Putting things in ink changes them from ideas to reality. When we see something written down, that thing becomes real. When we lay our eyes on the vision for our life, it is made possible in our mind. The vision Habakkuk was to record would serve as a marker or evidence for all to see.

Inscribe It on Tablets

The *New King James* version says this: "Make it plain on tablets." God definitely wanted the vision He gave Habakkuk to be legible for anyone to read. He wanted to make sure that no one would mistake the meaning of the vision. He wanted it ready so that Habakkuk could literally hand it to someone to read.

Wait for God to Give the Message

Though it tarries, wait for it. God knew that the vision would take some time. It wasn't for that day. It was for the future. God, in His goodness and love for Habakkuk, told him that the vision would come. If Habakkuk was confident in anything, it was in God's direct word and assurance that the vision was coming.

I had a dream that reached far beyond my grasp. I had a dream with no connections or celebrity status to help me. It was just my God and me. My sweet friend, what are you waiting for? I wonder what God has promised you today. If God has promised you something, it is on the way. Doubt it not! Stand and station yourself with a watchful eye! Your perfectly appointed time to see God's promise might become a reality sooner than you think.

But the righteous shall live by [her] faith (Hab. 2:4).

QUESTIONS THAT SEEK TRUTH

1. According to Isaiah 30:18, what does the Lord long to do for you?
2. As God waits on us, what are the four different actions He is waiting on us to perform?
3. Repentance, rest, quietness and trust are required for the Lord to bless you. Which one of these characteristics do you struggle with the most?
4. In this chapter what are two Bible stories in which God waited when He could have acted instantaneously?
5. There is an intentional reason for your wait. If you are waiting for something, what could God be doing behind the scenes?

6. Your waiting period will end. Why do you think it's so hard to wait expectantly?

7. Dependence, faith and long-suffering are just a few things God teaches us during a waiting period. When did you learn an important lesson because of the wait? What did you learn?

8. Are you aware that God is waiting with you while you are waiting? He sees all your emotion and longs to carry you through the wait. Can you think of a time when you felt His presence while waiting?

9. There is no time lost when God calls us to wait. Understanding that you are not missing out on a blessing because the time has not come is a perspective that is difficult to understand. Did you ever experience a time when someone looked down on you because you were waiting on a promise? Explain.

10. God's promise is as good as done. If you have to wait for 5 months or 50 years, if He has promised it, it will come. Is there a time when you did not believe that? Explain.

9

The Significance of Rejection

*Sometimes, I think a lot about the world existing without me,
and what it would be like.*

BLUSH ATTENDEE

Even when you are rejected and alone in the physical, you are totally accepted
by God. How does that knowledge affect your mark on the world?

If you have ever felt rejection to any degree, let me be the first to
welcome you to the rejection club. You have joined the rank of the
most highly influential people known to man. Your name will be
displayed beside Moses' name; he was rejected multiple times by
the entire nation of Israel. Who else is in the club? Joseph, whose
own brothers sold him into slavery; afterward, he became second
in command over all of Egypt. King David was rejected many times
and found himself running from King Saul, whom, at one time,
David had soothed out of dark moods by playing his harp. Then,
of course, there is Esther, who faced harsh rejection from Haman
and could have been killed by her own husband for standing up for
the Jewish people. Daniel was also rejected and placed in the lion's
den. Shadrach, Meshach and Abednego were thrown into the fiery
furnace. Paul, Peter, James, John . . . need I go on?

In modern times we've seen that people such as Abraham
Lincoln and Martin Luther King Jr. faced the ultimate rejection
for their beliefs, and their fight ended with death. Although all of
these people were amazing men and women, your name will also

fall in line with the name that is above every name, the King of kings, Jesus, who was despised and rejected by men. I have never been so proud to bear the label "rejected." Knowing that I am in the same company doesn't make me feel so bad after all!

At first I sat calmly in the pale blue room of the church I grew up in. The tables were positioned in a rectangle so that each of us in the room could see each other's face. This room, just a couple of years earlier, was the room where I put on my wedding dress to marry the man who now sat diagonally from me. The warm and inviting room that had boasted of joy and happiness just a couple of years earlier now seemed cold and dark. The fluorescent lighting made the room feel like an interrogation room for a criminal.

I sat in the middle of the rectangle and faced opposition—several men whom for my entire life I had looked up to. I had been to dinner at their homes, celebrated Christmases with their families, babysat their kids, was babysat by them and grew up knowing them as men who were substitute family. My dad was the pastor of the church I attended, but he was not allowed at this meeting. With all the strength I could muster on that spring night, I sat quietly, not speaking until spoken to. The meeting was part of the process of confronting me on filing for divorce.

At the time, this meeting seemed monumental to me; looking back now, God had me in that meeting for a much greater purpose. The details of the divorce had been discussed with the church leadership because I was the pastor's daughter and had received support from the leadership for a short time. That night, however, the tide had turned. I could feel my face grow hot, and the nerves in my body were tense. My pulse sounded like a drum in my ear loud enough to distract me for a time.

The meeting began with prayer. As we prayed, God reminded me where I stood with Him. This momentary act of human rejection was nothing like the acceptance I had received in my relationship with Him. As the meeting began, I dreaded going through the agenda. Futile things were discussed, such as property division and the explanation of meaningless conversations. The leadership listened to my replies as I explained my actions. I knew what God had spoken to me, and for the first time in my life, I would not be persuaded to do anything against His plan for me.

I had made horrible decisions that went completely against His plan for my life; but as I sat in that room, I was now confident of the direction God had called me to go. None of my answers seemed good enough. The rebuttal from a couple of the men was strong and convincing. After a while, I just sat in silence as the firing squad continued. I looked down at the old 10-foot table and tried to pick the plastic from the edge. I was at a loss. I looked for comfort from my youth pastor, sitting to my right, but I found none as he stared ahead as if fixated on an object on the wall to distract him. There I sat, alone, when the chairman of the deacon board picked up a large book from the floor. I didn't recognize the book, so I was interested in what it would say. He said, "You are planning on attending Liberty University in the fall, correct?" "Yes," I answered. He responded with, "Do you know what they think about divorce?" "Not really," I said. He then opened up the book and read the biblical stance that Liberty University took on divorce and said, "Do you think they are going to accept you?"

I was floored by that unexpected move and responded with a yes. The chairman of the deacons didn't know that my father had called Jerry Falwell, the founder of Liberty University, just a few days earlier and asked for his advice. Jerry Falwell was a friend of my grandparents when they grew up in Lynchburg, Virginia. As a family friend, Jerry would regularly take my dad's calls. Jerry's response after hearing the entire story of my situation went something like this: "You tell that girl to get in a car and get to Liberty University and find her a man who will love her like Christ loves His church." Coming from such a man of God, this had again confirmed my act of obedience.

I didn't tell them that night about my father's conversation with Jerry Falwell, but I sat there and simply responded with a yes.

After that, this man looked me squarely in the eyes and said, "If you do this, if you go through with this divorce, God will never use you." I didn't listen to anything that was said the rest of the night. But I have never forgotten that line: "God will never use you." When the meeting concluded, I stood up, pushed my chair under the table and walked to my car. On the brisk drive home that evening, God reminded me of the people He used whose stories were recorded in Scripture. He began to remind me of the total screw-ups He had made into champions for His name. I drove away that night rejected and alone in the physical, but accepted in the heavenly.

Let's Get Real

This was one of my harshest stories of rejection, but let me be clear: That night, God used that group of men to teach me many things that would take me a lifetime to learn if it hadn't happened. The severity of rejection I faced from those men taught me things that I use to this day to deal with rejection when it comes. In those two-plus hours of intense pain, God wrote the wisdom of how to deal with rejection on my heart.

> He was despised and rejected by men; a man of sorrows, and acquainted with grief: and as one from whom men hide their faces he was despised, and we esteemed him not (Isa. 53:3, *ESV*).

Even when our rejection is severe, it is nothing compared to the rejection the Lord Jesus bore.

Jesus Was Rejected in His Hometown

> And He said, "Truly I say to you, no prophet is welcome in his hometown" (Luke 4:24).

Jesus felt the sting of rejection where He grew up in Nazareth. It was there that He chose to stand in the synagogue and read two verses from the prophet Isaiah (Isa. 61:1-2) and told them He had come to fulfill those verses (see Luke 4:21). When the people of Nazareth, the very place where Jesus was raised—His stomping ground—heard His teaching after reading the verses, they got up and drove Him out of the city and led Him to the brow of the hill on which their city had been built in order to throw Him down the cliff (see vv. 26-30).

The people in Nazareth didn't understand who Jesus was and what He was doing. The Bible says that the people were "filled with rage" (v. 26). They did not accept Him, and they drove Him out.

I have taken great comfort in knowing that my Jesus understood what it was like for me that night as I took the verbal bullets one by one. He sat there with me on that chair and comforted me because He knew what it was to be rejected by those He grew up with.

The deacons at my church decided to move me to church discipline (which meant they decided that I was not welcome at the church any longer). That phone call was one of the darkest days of my life. My church had decided I wasn't welcome, even though I was being abused in my marriage. I pulled my membership from the church and started anew.

Just because Jesus was rejected by His hometown does not mean that He didn't have a significant plan for His life. He didn't call it quits; He moved on to where God had Him go next. His rejection by His hometown did not disable Him; it moved Him forward in His mission.

Jesus Was Rejected by His Close Confidants

Immediately, while He was still speaking, Judas, one of the twelve, came up accompanied by a crowd with swords and clubs, who were from the chief priests and the scribes and the elders. Now he who was betraying Him had given them a signal, saying, "Whomever I kiss, He is the one; seize Him and lead Him away under guard" (Mark 14:43-44).

Judas Iscariot was one of Jesus' 12 disciples. He had walked with Jesus for some time and knew Jesus intimately. He saw Jesus do many miracles and listened to all the teachings that thousands were amazed by. He saw the physical and spiritual healings of the blind, the lame and the sick. He was there through it all. And though Jesus knew that Judas was going to betray Him, I imagine it was quite a difficult moment for Jesus in the garden of Gethsemane, staring at a man who had walked with Him the past few years and laughed and eaten and joked with Him. A man whom Jesus loved chose to turn his back on Him.

I know that you can relate to this. Most of us have been betrayed by someone comfortable enough with us to kiss us. It's a pain that many of us feel, but we think no one can understand. Well, Jesus gets it. He felt it. Whatever close loved one has rejected you, He's been there too. God pieced the Bible together to be relatable to us, and He knew that we would have days when someone close to us would decide to reject us. He is walking with you through your rejection. Do not feel like you are alone in this. The nausea that immediately hits you when you find out what has been done to you behind your back is a common response. The fear that seems to plague you when you are in other relationships is familiar. The tendency to fight back is normal. However, rejection teaches us dependence on the Lord, and putting up a wall of defense will paralyze the lesson. We learn that men (or women) will betray and disappoint, but God never will.

Jesus Was Rejected by Those He Came to Save

> So they cried out, "Away with Him, away with Him, crucify Him!" Pilate said, "Shall I crucify your King?" The chief priests answered, "We have no king but Caesar." So he then handed Him over to them to be crucified (John 19:15-16).

The very people whom Jesus was helping—healing their sicknesses, raising their dead, doing amazing miracles in front of them—rejected Him. They chose to beat, torture and kill the very man who was going to give them eternal life. The rejection of an entire body of people, after He had shepherded them, must have been colossally painful.

I want to speak for a moment to those of you who are leaders. This can be moms, dads, pastors and older siblings—anyone who shepherds others. The rejection you feel when you have been rejected by those you have diligently cared for is a pain you have to feel to understand. You may be a mom whose child has turned his or her back on you; you may be a wife whose husband has had an affair. Pastor, has your congregation gone behind your back and gossiped about you to the extreme point of calling for your resignation? Leader, has your staff member quit due to reckless information? I know the pain of being rejected by the ones I have poured myself into, and let me encourage you with this, you have experienced the fellowship of our Lord Jesus' sufferings.

> That I may know Him and the power of His resurrection and the fellowship of His sufferings, being conformed to His death; in order that I may attain to the resurrection from the dead (Phil. 3:10-11).

Because of your experience with rejection, you have received a closer and more intimate look at what Jesus felt like the day that all those He cared for and came to serve shouted, "Crucify Him!" There have been times when I have felt like I was being flogged emotionally. My soul cried out with each lash. Pain that I wish no one would ever have to feel has permeated my heart. It is in those times that I have realized I do not stand alone. When tempted to isolate myself, Jesus looks at me and lovingly says, *I am here.* He says the same to you: "Come to me, all who are weary and heavy laden, and I will give you rest" (Matt. 11:28). *I am waiting with my arms open wide and I accept you. I will never let you go.*

There is no comfort like that of a God who has been through the trial of rejection. You cannot find a more secure acceptance than with a God who sees the injustice and runs to give you aid. Jesus' response was so beautiful on the cross when He said, "Father, forgive them; for they do not know what they are doing" (Luke 23:34).

Jesus Felt Rejection by God

> About the ninth hour Jesus cried out with a loud voice, saying, "ELI, ELI, LAMA SABACHTHANI? that is, "MY GOD, MY GOD, WHY HAVE YOU FORSAKEN ME?" (Matt. 27:46).

Jesus felt the deepest rejection by God as He hung on the cross that day. Hanging there, alone, bearing the sins of the whole world, His inner thoughts came pouring forth in a statement of the utmost grief. Jesus' feelings of abandonment by His Father leave me speechless even as I type these words. I could never attempt to convey the depth of His feelings. My mind fails me when I think of a Savior who would love me enough to be rejected by every form of support that is possible. I stand in awe of Him.

> My God, my God why have You forsaken me? Far from my deliverance are the words of my groaning. O my God, I cry by day, but You do not answer; and by night, but I have no rest. Yet You are holy, O You who are enthroned upon the praises of Israel (Ps. 22:1-3).

Notice David's use of the exact words Jesus said while on the cross. The feeling of rejection is one that is almost unbearable. I bring this point to the surface of Jesus' feeling abandoned and rejected by His Father because the idea that God had rejected me is one that I struggled with for a long time. Only 12 years ago, I remember feeling that God hated me and wanted me dead. I remember the thoughts that plagued my mind. I believed that God had rejected me because of my decisions, because of my sin and because of my past. I couldn't process the knowledge of a God who forgave, because I had done so much wrong. In the deepest, darkest place of sin that I wallowed in, He was there waiting for me to choose Him.

I want you to know, whatever your sin, whatever your mistakes, whatever you represent, He is waiting for you with His arms open wide. He is ready for you to run to Him and feel the acceptance you long for.

When I went to Liberty University, I was struggling with guilt. I forced my family to suffer things they were no part of. My sin had caused harsh consequences for all those around me. I was in a psychology class my first semester at Liberty, and after class I had a conversation with an older lady in the class and told her, "I am really struggling with guilt; does God really accept my apology?" I will never forget what she said: "Autumn, don't you ever be too prideful to think that Jesus' blood didn't cover your sin." That was all it took. Feeling that God has rejected you is common, but it is just a feeling. Be aware that what you are feeling is a false sense of reality. The Bible clearly tells us over and over that He will never leave us nor forsake us. You must fight the feeling of being forsaken by God, because it is not fact. The fact is, He walks with you.

Possible Side Effects from Rejection

You May Question Who You Are

Satan capitalizes on the rejection and starts putting thoughts in our mind, such as, *Are they right?* or *Do I have something wrong with me?* We must combat this side effect with God's Word.

Truth:

> But now listen, O Jacob, My servant, And Israel, whom I have chosen: Thus says the LORD who made you and formed you from the womb, who will help you, "Do not fear, O Jacob My servant; and you Jeshurun whom I have chosen" (Isa. 44:1-2).

You May Question the Call of God on Your Life

The enemy wants nothing more than for you to start questioning exactly what God has asked you to do. It is so important that we stay confident in His call through confirmation of His Word before we take a step forward in that call. If God has confirmed the call when people reject you because of it, you can continually go back to the confirmation and stand on that promise. When God told me and confirmed to me that I was going to start a traveling conference ministry, He gave me the passage from Habakkuk 2: 2-4. This was the greatest thing He could have done for me, because whenever I begin to question my call, I can go back to that passage and it reminds me of my clear directive from the Lord. The only word that matters is the Lord's.

> Who has saved us and called us with a holy calling, not according to our works, but according to His own purpose and grace which was granted us in Christ Jesus from all eternity (2 Tim. 1:9).

You May React with Super-Charged Emotions

It is so hard not to react when people accuse you and reject you for reasons you feel are not valid; but I urge you to give the Lord charge over your emotions. Ask Him, as David did in Psalm 141, to lock the door of your lips.

Set a guard, O LORD, over my mouth; Keep watch over the door of my lips (Ps. 141:3).

Your job when feeling rejected is to lean into the most Mighty Support, not react in a way that would scar His name. In this age of social media, I can read my news feeds and know the people who are feeling rejected. Their feelings are everywhere. Check your super-charged emotions and rely on the Lord. When we handle rejection well, the benefits far exceed the side effects.

Face Your Deepest Rejection and Find Your Greatest Acceptance

Rejection is significant in the Christian life, because to fight the victorious fight of faith, we will face rejection. Understanding that Jesus experienced every form of it should tell us that we will face it regularly.

If the world hates you, you know that it has hated Me before it hated you (John 15:18).

Without facing rejection, I didn't have a need to find acceptance. Before facing severe rejection, I searched for acceptance regularly. But the acceptance I was getting was not the kind I needed. The shallow acceptance I was receiving was masking a deeper need I had to be accepted; and when the high of the temporal acceptance wore off, I would run to find it again. Man's applause and compliments were all things that would wear off after only a short time. However, when all were silenced and none of them were available to ease my urge to be accepted, I found exactly what I was longing for in my God. His acceptance is like none I have ever known in people. He made me exactly who I am, so I don't need to explain why I am so loud and crazy: because He made me that way. I don't have to explain any desires to Him, because He already knows why He put them there. With Him, I can be me—no charade, no fancy talk needed. He isn't impressed by it anyway.

The rejection I have faced on earth pales in comparison to the abundant acceptance I have found in my relationship with my

Savior. If it weren't for the rejection, I wouldn't have found that acceptance. God allows us to feel the sting of it to bring us to a closer, more intimate relationship with Him. When I surrendered my heart to Him and He dealt kindly with it and didn't mistreat it, He gave me hope to go deeper in my relationship with Him. The deeper I went, the more accepted I felt. Every good thing in me is a result of His taking this shattered heart and piecing it back together.

Sweet friend, I know that you are reading this while feeling the sting of rejection from a parent, a friend or a spouse; and it has hit you hard. I know that kind of rejection. So let me tell you that without the acceptance I found in my Jesus, I would have no confidence in my call. The same can be true for you. Find your acceptance in Jesus, and He will affirm the call He has on your life.

QUESTIONS THAT SEEK THE TRUTH

1. Name a giant of the Christian faith who was rejected. How does that make you feel?

2. Jesus' life gives us the best example of being rejected by people. He was rejected first by His hometown. Did you ever feel rejected by your inner circle growing up? Describe that time.

3. Judas, a man Jesus mentored, exemplified rejection of the worst kind. Why was his behavior so despicable? When has there been a time when someone you have helped betrayed you?

4. In John 19:6, the Jews screamed, "Crucify Him!" about Jesus. Have you ever found yourself in a situation when you felt the world was against you? What were the circumstances?

5. When Jesus hung on the cross, He felt the reality of God's rejection. Scripture records, "He made Him who new no sin to be sin on our behalf, so that we might become the righteousness of God in Him." Based on this truth, what can you glean as true from those times when you have felt lonely, isolated and forsaken by God? How does it speak to your sense of significance?

6. Rejection comes with side effects that, if not dealt with, can steal our sense of significance. We begin to question who we are. When have you struggled with your identity because of rejection? What makes the most sense to you now about who you are?

7. Does it seem as if when you are working toward your purpose you are continually getting rejected? What do you make of that?

8. Super-charged emotions can derail us when we don't look for the purpose behind our rejection. Has there been a time when this has happened to you? How did you get back on track?

9. Rejection is significant because it is in that place that we find our greatest acceptance. Has there been a time when, even though everyone around you rejected you, you found acceptance with the Lord?

10. Confidence in the Lord can stand firm even when others reject you. That confidence and stability are paramount in achieving what God has for you. When have you seen that truth become reality for you?

10

The Significance of Tenacity

The number one lie Satan tells me is that I have no significance.

BLUSH ATTENDEE

Why is tenacity a key attitude when answering God's call?

The first time someone told me I was tenacious, I had no idea what it meant, nor did I know how to spell it. I said thank you with a smirk on my face and then went home and looked up the word. When I read the definition, I laughed out loud because it perfectly described me.

When the Lord confirmed through His Word that He wanted me to start to develop a traveling conference ministry, I began to pray relentlessly about the details. I prayed for 10 years about the launch of The Blush Network. The longer the vision tarried, the more steadfast I became in praying. The time that elapsed didn't deter me or discourage me, because I knew without a doubt that this was what God wanted for my life.

I prayed every way one can pray. God gave me the grace to power through those days when Satan's influence of discouragement was heavy on me. Prayer became my food during that season because I knew one day my waiting period for the vision God had given me would be over.

You can be tenacious about many things, but nothing is as important to be tenacious about as God's calling on your life. When you are not resolute on exactly what God wants you to do, many things are at stake, such as leading others toward salvation, your own spiritual growth and helping to redirect wayward people back to Christ.

One of my most precious callings is to be a mother. I will not take for granted the fact that God gave me children to care for and raise to serve Him so that they can accomplish what He wants for their lives. Whatever God's callings for your life, you must be persistent about focusing on them.

When we are lazy, lethargic or unintentional about our lives, and we don't grasp the fact that we are here for a purpose and have spiritual tasks to complete, we miss out on the miraculous, and Satan wins.

After trashing seven years of my life, I made a conscious decision that I was not going to live for myself any longer. My weak sense of purpose for my life got me divorced at the age of 22; God's significant purposes for my life allowed me to get married to an amazing man, parent beautiful children, and run a ministry that is reaching thousands for the Lord each year. See the difference? Tenacity for the things of God will pay off. What the world says or thinks is irrelevant compared to pleasing God.

God is tenacious about His will to have a relationship with us. That's why He sent His Son as a sacrifice for our sins. Satan is also tenacious about achieving his own will and will do whatever he can to stop you from accomplishing what God has for you.

The lazy Christian life is ineffective for the Kingdom. Therefore, we must be warriors who are ready to power through any discouragement from the enemy in order to fulfill God's call on our lives. A song I used to sing in church, as a kid, contains the powerful words "I'm in the Lord's army." Well, we can't just sing it; we need to act it out. God needs each of us to be a warrior who is ready to fight for His cause at any given time.

There have been several times when I have received a call and knew that I needed to go "Gangsta Jesus" in prayer on behalf of the person on the other end. Be aware that Satan wants to devour us, especially when we are taking a huge step of faith. Assuming the position of a warrior and not turning around and running in fear is the only way to take this nation back. We don't have the option of being weak Christians in today's world.

I don't want to go to church to get entertained; I want to go to church to meet with Jesus. I don't need a sermon on how to have a better sex life with my husband; I need to know how to fight today's culture with the power of God. I don't want a message from a great orator; I want a message from the Holy Spirit.

Let's Get Real

Tenacity is important when faith is challenged, but most times it isn't our natural inclination. There is a reason that we battle feelings of wanting to quit when things get difficult. We are flesh, and in ourselves we are not equipped to handle high stress, discouragement or the frustrating situations we will meet when in the center of God's will for our lives. The natural self desires to give in when the odds seem too hard to overcome. You may be strong for a while, but the phrase "the straw that broke the camel's back" ends up causing you to give in.

When the walls start falling in on your calling, but you know that God has been clear about the direction for your life, you must stand strong in the strength of the Lord. Your eyes must rise above the mess you see yourself in and focus on the prize set before you. God will not let you to be overcome; you have the power to be tenacious even when you can't feel it. Power is available to you when the Spirit of God resides in you. After all, it's God's job to overcome the enormous roadblocks, not yours.

The apostle Paul knew the importance of pressing on in the midst of hardship. Empowered by the Holy Spirit, he wrote these encouraging words about tenacity:

> Therefore, we do not lose heart, but though our outer man is decaying, yet our inner man is being renewed day by day. For momentary, light affliction is producing for us an eternal weight of glory far beyond all comparison, while we look not at the things which are seen, but at the things which are not seen; for the things which are seen are temporal, but the things which are not seen are eternal (2 Cor. 4:16-18).

Even though the outer man (our body) is decaying, we can be renewed day by day. We have to choose to be renewed day by day.

The renewing process comes from time spent with the Lord. You cannot be renewed spiritually and be ready for hardship without that renewal. Tenacity in your significance is only possible with constant refreshing from our Lord.

Paul goes on to speak in verse 18 of looking at the things that are not seen. When tragedy hits as we press on toward our calling, we must lift our eyes from that situation to the Lord and understand that the situation is a short season; it will be over soon; our purpose will continue. But wrapping ourselves in the drama of our circumstances will crush the opportunity to achieve our significance.

I was ecstatic after the first conference for The Blush Network. I felt as though I could have taken on anything. I saw the hand of God show up so beautifully. He literally paved the way in the desert, just like His Word says He will do.

In 2009, I could feel the Lord begin to speak to my spirit and continue to tell me to get ready. I prayed heavily about the name Blush. For years, I had no idea what I would name the ministry. I knew that God would give me the name, and I was willing to wait until He saw fit. One day, during my devotional time, I looked down at my Bible and felt the Lord say to my spirit, *Blush*. I had been praying for a name that wasn't too churchy, because I wanted to minister to the un-churched; but I also wanted it to be feminine. I knew immediately that Blush was our name. I added "Network" to the end because I knew that Blush wouldn't be only a conference ministry. We have now added small groups, devotionals, single-night events and leadership training. God has truly blessed our growth.

After God spoke to my spirit about the name Blush, I immediately moved to action. Just a month later, I completed the first Blush devotional and began to blog using that name. After our first conference, the delight of having launched a 10-year vision overwhelmed me. We set up a bank account and got a P.O. box. Things were finally clicking as we filed our paperwork with the government and began the journey to become a 501(c)3.

One day, I stopped by the post office, grabbed the mail and got back in the car. But before starting the engine, I opened a letter that puzzled me a little because it was from another ministry named Blush. It was a cease and desist letter. They politely told me to drop the name Blush and use something else because they owned the rights. I immediately called my husband and said, "Can this be true? What are we going to do?"

I knew that I didn't steal the name from anywhere. I knew that God had given it to me, but apparently they didn't. I began to freak out. My whole cloud nine experience seemed to become a horrible rainy day in one second. I began thinking of all the "what ifs." At this point, we had so much marketing, money and time into the name, and I was petrified at what this could mean. This was a giant test of my faith. I immediately turned my attention to seek the Lord. I cried out His Word and His promises, asking Him to work this out.

Well, a short time later, we received another letter. I was hoping it would go away, but it didn't. Still seeking the Lord, I started praying differently. I began to tell the Lord that this wasn't my problem; it was His. He was the One who called me to this ministry and gave me this name, so He had to work on our behalf to figure this out. I could feel the need to act; I just didn't know how. When another letter showed up, I was at my wits' end. I had prayed every way I knew how, and still I sat there not knowing what to do.

In my devotional time the next day, I begged God to work, and then I received an email. I opened it while in my devotional time. It was from a friend, who wrote, "I was thinking of you and wanted to share a verse with you. God put you on my heart."

> Do not fear, for I am with you; do not anxiously look about you, for I am your God. I will strengthen you, surely I will help you, surely I will uphold you with My righteous right hand (Isa. 41:10).

I almost fell out of my chair. I immediately picked up the phone and called her. She loved that God used her in such a way, and as I explained what we were going through, she listened and then said, "I may know someone who could help." That led to a contact who just happened to be one of the top attorneys in the country for intellectual property. He agreed to take our case pro bono.

During the process of gathering evidence that we possessed the name first, there were days when discouragement plagued me. I remember one specific day when I was looking through my email to prove that we used the name first. I wept on the floor and told God that whatever He wanted was what I wanted. Whatever He wanted was okay with me, because I knew He would take care of it. I grabbed my Bible and flipped it open to Psalm 37.

> Commit your way to the LORD, trust also in Him, and He will do it (Ps. 37:5).

I read this verse with a new understanding. It was life giving. It was my opportunity to stand on that promise of God. In that moment, on that floor, I chose to forget my circumstances and believe that God was speaking straight to me. I claimed His power over the situation; and with all the faith and tenacity I had, I reminded God of His promise. I realized that God was truly in control, and if I surrendered to what He wanted, I couldn't go wrong.

He has kept His promise. The Blush Network's growth skyrocketed after that point. It wasn't because of me; it was because of God's faithfulness. When we release the things we hold dear and trust God's goodness over them, He never fails.

I have adopted one of Joshua's lines in the Bible. He stated in Numbers 14:9, "For they will be our prey."

Joshua and Caleb were two completely normal people, like you and me, but their mindset of God's power motivated them. In Numbers 13, we see God telling Moses to send 12 spies into the land of Canaan, which is known as the Promised Land for the nation of Israel. After leading them from their captivity in Egypt, Moses led the nation of Israel to the border of Canaan. Twelve men were chosen, one from each tribe, to enter the land and assess it.

The men were chosen to spy out the land even though in Deuteronomy 1:8 we see God saying, "See, I have placed this land before you; go in and possess the land which the LORD swore to give to your fathers, to Abraham, to Isaac, and to Jacob, to them and to their descendants after them."

Deuteronomy 1:21-22 is especially telling:

> See, the LORD your God has placed this land before you; go up, take possession, as the LORD, the God of you Fathers, has spoken to you. Do not fear or be dismayed.

Then all of you approached me and said, "Let us send men before us, that they may search out the land for us, and bring back to us word of the way by which we should go up and the cities which we shall enter."

God told the nation of Israel that He was bringing them out of the bondage of Egypt and leading them to the Promised Land since Pharaoh from Egypt released them; yet, they needed to go in themselves and spy. They wanted to send humans in to spy the land when the Lord had already spied it for them. I get so frustrated by verse 22, where Moses says, "Then all of you approached me" and they asked him to send humans into the land of promise to look it over before they, as a whole, went in. They didn't have enough faith to enter the land based on God's promise to them; it wasn't good enough for them. They thought they needed to check up on God to see if His story checked out.

As frustrated as I get with this part of the story, I realize that we all do the same thing. How many times has God asked you to do something but you waited to see if God really wanted you to do it? You called everyone you know for confirmation of what God has already told you. Don't get me wrong, seeking godly counsel is biblical, but in your heart, you know what God has said, and sometimes you don't need counsel to obey. Delayed obedience is disobedience.

I have seen people who, resolute in the call of God on them, have sought too much counsel and become confused. They have ended up following the counsel rather than the voice of the Lord. When God gives you a task, pray and ask Him whose counsel you should seek. When He reveals the person, that person will give you the same counsel the Lord has given.

I know that your desire is to live a life that reaches all of its potential; so don't get caught up in the opinion of man when God's opinion of you is at stake.

God's Promises Are Absolute

God does not need our help or our perspective. If God says, "Go and possess the land," that is all we need. It is not our job to add our perspective to the mighty God's. This is such a temptation for us. Fitting our own agenda into God's plan is not following God's plan; we are making a new plan for ourselves. When God tells us to do something, we often want to question the why and the how. It has to make sense humanly speaking in order for us to feel confident doing it. That is not faith. Faith is saying, *Okay, God, I will follow. If I need to possess the land, I believe You have my back.* It amazes me how often we waver, even when we have been promised success, because our faith fails and we apply our human reasoning to His sovereign plan.

God's Promises Are Yours to Claim

Just as the nation of Israel had the promise of success in the land of Canaan, so too we have thousands of promises in the Bible to claim. I fear that we have forgotten that God has literally promised us success, help, power, forgiveness, salvation and provision, yet we live our lives as if we are defeated. Do you understand that the power of God is waiting for you to believe Him? With God's powerful promises on your side, you are assured success, just like the nation of Israel. We are more than conquerors in Him; His promises are true and trustworthy. He is the same God yesterday, today and forever. His promises you can take to the bank every time.

> Not one of the good promises which the LORD had made to the house of Israel failed: all came to pass (Josh. 21:45).

Do Not Take No for an Answer When
God Has Already Told You Yes

The 12 spies went into the land of Canaan and it was just as God had said. It flowed with milk and honey. The spies even cut down some grapes, pomegranates and figs to show the nation of Israel that it was indeed a good land; but their next breath was fatal.

> Nevertheless the people who live in the land are strong, and the cities are fortified and very large; and moreover, we saw the descendants of Anak there. . . . But the men who had gone up with him [Caleb] said, "We are not able

to go up against the people, for they are too strong for us"
(Num. 13:28,31).

Ten of the 12 men who went into the land to assess it accepted
defeat even though God promised them victory. They put their
spin on the situation and eventually convinced the entire nation
that God was in fact a liar and they would not be successful. Were
there obstacles in the land of Canaan? Yes, but God had told them
they would have victory.

This passage is sobering. I never want to be like the 10 men who
saw the very hand of God roll back the waters of the Red Sea and
feed them with manna and quail without end, and yet they were at
a point where they had to exercise faith but couldn't. If God tells
you yes, do not take no for an answer.

We must not accept no if God says go. We do not know what is
on the other side of that yes. Your Promised Land could be waiting
for you, but the catch is that giants surround it.

Your Feelings Rarely Represent Fact

The 10 men were relying solely on their feelings when they brought
dismay to the nation of Israel through a bad report. They felt helpless, and they probably were without the help of the Lord. We get
into trouble when we constantly rely on our wavering feelings.
Feelings often lie to us about the facts. Our feelings, especially
as women, can be unreliable. We have hormones and all sorts of
crazy things going on each month that can alter the truth. When a
sentence starts with the words "I feel," I immediately engage with
"You may feel that way, but what is truth?"

We take our feelings too seriously, and it leads us to forgoing
some of the most amazing things that God may have for us. I have
often heard, "I feel inadequate to do this for God." Well, if God
doesn't think you are inadequate, then believe Him. We must push
through the romanticism of feelings and accept that God may call
us to something far beyond the realm of our imagination if we
cease to give our feelings power.

There have been many days when I have felt stupid, sinful, inadequate, uneducated and hopeless. I may feel that way, but when
God looks at me, He sees a tenacious and willing spirit He wants to

use. So I have accepted His opinion. I'm going with God's feelings and not mine.

Don't Let Discouragement Stop You

The steroids we inject into our discouragement fuel our disobedience. Joshua and Caleb saw the same things the other 10 men saw. They saw that the people of Canaan were huge and that the cities were strong. I'm sure they were tempted to give in to discouragement just like the other guys did, but they didn't.

There are days when I feel as though the task at hand is just too great. Satan tempts me to believe that things are going to be too difficult to overcome, and I can feel myself beginning to creep into the pit of discouragement. That's when I run to God's Word. God's Word is the best antidote for discouragement. Using God's Word effectively is using it to battle our tough days. Many times, I have come to His Word and in just one verse I have felt encouraged. His Word is power, and there is no way we overcome the temptation of discouragement without it.

Friends or family will never offer the life-giving hope that Scripture will. When you are discouraged, you need to go immediately to the Bible rather than to anything else. The words of Ephesians 6:17 tell us to take up the sword of the Spirit, which is the Word of God. The Bible itself is a weapon of offense. It will minister to you when no one and nothing else can.

Joshua and Caleb remembered that God had said, "See, the LORD your God has placed this land before you; go up, take possession, as the LORD, the God of your fathers, has spoken to you. Do not fear or be dismayed" (Deut. 1:21). Their perspective on the odds of victory was based on that.

The Bible Never Says It's Okay to Quit

When Joshua and Caleb saw the revolt of the nation of Israel after the other 10 spies reported, they spoke up and said:

> The land which we passed through to spy out is an exceedingly good land. If the LORD is pleased with us, then He will bring us into this land and give it to us—a land which flows with milk and honey. Only do not rebel against the LORD;

and do not fear the people of the land, for they will be
our prey. Their protection has been removed from them,
and the LORD is with us; do not fear them (Num. 14:7-9).

Joshua and Caleb saw the value in pressing forward even
in the midst of hard circumstances. The very fulfillment of the
promise was at stake, and they knew they had no choice but to
trust the Lord. I have sat across the table from many a leader
who is ready to quit. One particular time, I felt this sweet person's pain. I understood the desperate situation the person was
in and wanted to take the pain for myself; however, I knew that
God wasn't done with this person and I leaned close and said,
"Nowhere in the Bible does it ever say you can quit." The Bible
screams the opposite; in Joshua 1, God tells Joshua over and over
to be strong and courageous. I have put the words of Joshua 1:9
on my refrigerator at home.

Have I not commanded you? Be strong and courageous!
Do not tremble or be dismayed, for the LORD your God
is with you wherever you go (Josh. 1:9).

Every day those words remind me to not fear or accept defeat,
but to lean on Him.

Your Calling Will Be Surrounded by Attack

Moses died, and Joshua went on to lead the nation of Israel. He was
definitely tested in this story to lean into the power of God and
not give in to the pressure of peers or to his feelings. His reward
was great for tenaciously trusting in the word of the Lord; and as
it played out later in Scripture, He led the Israelites in defeating
those powerful cities, one by one. The Israelite nation had to fight
the cities, but just as the Lord had said, they were victorious, little
by little, until they possessed the entire land of Canaan.

The other 10 men weren't allowed to enter the Promised Land,
and they died in the wilderness. What an opportunity they lost!
Because of their doubt and their destructive report, they didn't
enter the land of Canaan, nor did the grumbling portion of Israel.

They came to a moment when they had to stand on the word of the Lord, but they chose not to. We, in the same way, have those moments of truth. We can tenaciously say, "They will be our prey," or we can say, "They are more mighty than we are." Tenacity is an imperative because your significant calling will be surrounded by attack. The enemy will attack you as you begin to assume your calling, and he will attack you when you achieve it.

There has never been a day when I have regretted standing on the word of the Lord. When I tenaciously fought for the ground that God promised to give me more than 10 years ago, I had a front-row seat to the miraculous. I have literally seen God part the impossible Red Sea in front of me, over and over again. Tenacity is a necessary component to be a warrior of the King.

QUESTIONS THAT SEEK TRUTH

1. Tenacity is important when faith is challenged, but it doesn't come naturally. What is your definition of tenacity?
2. Joshua said, in Numbers 14:9, "They will be our prey." He exercised his tenacity when the nation of Israel wanted to give in. When have you been the only one in your group to exercise tenacity?
3. The Lord told the nation of Israel that He would give them success even before they sent spies into the land of Canaan. What future thing has God told you that you would have success in accomplishing?
4. If God says, "Take the land," He means just that. He does not need you to qualify His directive. When have you acted on your own perspective rather than God's directive and experienced defeat?
5. The 10 spies accepted defeat although God promised victory. When have you or someone you know accepted defeat instead of victory?
6. Why is accepting victory from God difficult?
7. Our feelings rarely represent fact, but we act on feelings as fact and find out that we have been foolish to do so. What is the difference between feeling and fact?

8. The steroids we inject into our discouragement fuel our disobedience. Joshua and Caleb saw the exact same thing that the other 10 spies saw. Why was their perspective different from the others'?

9. Quitting is never an option when you are living a life of purpose. Can you remember a time when you quit but have always wondered what could have been? What would you do differently now if you had the opportunity?

10. Your significance will always be surrounded by attack. Joshua's tenacity qualified him as a candidate to lead Israel, and that's what he ultimately did. What can your tenacity do for you?

11

The Significance of Forgiveness

Unforgiveness deprives me of peace—you carry that weight for years. Sometimes you can't forgive yourself.

BLUSH ATTENDEE

What does your lack of forgiveness deprive you of, and how does it harm the world?

I have wanted to adopt a child since I was in high school. I could almost picture the infant child, with dark hair and eyes, who would one day be in my family, if God allowed it.

My desire to adopt sometimes puzzled me. When I married the second time, my husband, Eddie Miles, and I talked at length about it. Once our daughter, Grace, was born, and then our son, Jude, we felt like we were complete with our biological children. But we knew that if we were to have any more children, we would adopt.

I will never forget the day my husband arrived home after attending a conference in Atlanta and looked at me and said, "Now is the time to adopt." I burst into tears because the Lord had finally given him direction on the timing to add to our family. I wasted no time. Adoption is extremely expensive, so I began to pray for God to provide the expenses needed to make it a reality. Within one week of praying, God provided 100 percent of the funds needed to move forward. We were stunned at the provision of the Lord.

We immediately started the rigorous adoption process. Some days, I felt slightly invaded, as they wanted every piece of information about all four of us. The day we sent our paperwork off was a day for the history books. I remember driving to the UPS store knowing that our baby was on the way. When we handed the clerk the manila envelope with all of our information, we captured the moment with a picture. We left confident of the calling on our family's life.

That January, we joined the list of hopeful waiting parents. With every opportunity to get picked to be adoptive parents my heart soared with the excitement of what if. We knew that each time a mother looked at our profile there was a good possibility that she would pick us. Days turned into months as we waited. Each no from a birth mom came hard and pushed me to my knees in prayer. Some days I would weep under the rejection, and some days I would champion it with faith. The desire for a third child was not going away; it was multiplying.

After several months of waiting, we received a phone call from our representative at the adoption agency while we were eating ice cream after my children's first day of school. My cookie dough ice cream sundae with caramel sauce slowly melted as I rushed to answer my ringing phone. I stared straight into Eddie's eyes as our representative told us there was a birth mother who wanted to speak with us. We had received several opportunities the previous week, and I was anxiously awaiting the name of the birth mother so that I could understand what we were looking at. When I asked our representative for the name and she told me, I burst out in loud laughter because this was the birth mother who was pregnant with twins. Not letting her continue, I stopped the conversation to quickly tell Eddie that this was the mom with twins. Just a week earlier, we had laughed when we were profiled to a mom pregnant with twins, because we thought she would pick us. And she did.

We anxiously waited for the phone call the next day. The birth mother was going to call at noon sharp because she had further questions for us. The idea of waiting by the phone took on a whole new meaning for us as we sat there in case she would call early. The phone rang, and our conversation went seamlessly, and the birth mother said, "My heart is so happy." I couldn't believe how well the conversation went.

As exciting as it was, my heart was not at rest. I had no idea why. This was the opportunity I had waited for. This was the moment I had dreamed of for so many years; yet I didn't have peace. I quickly justified it away as feelings of anxiety because it was twins and not a single baby. Surely that was the reason for the check in my spirit.

Time went on and my work took me to Atlanta. The birth mother was from Atlanta, and I had been counseled to see if she would meet with us. She was so quick to say, "Of course," and we would figure out details when the date got closer. Well, the day came and, lo and behold, we were told this birth mother's aunt had died. I was extremely disappointed, but I tried to be understanding because I knew she needed to be with her family.

When we left Atlanta, the spirit inside of me began to scream. I had been given the birth mother's information along with an ultrasound, but I had only looked at it on my phone. The Tuesday morning after we returned from Atlanta, I felt the Lord say to me, "Investigate." I got my computer and began to do some research on this particular birth mother. I found her picture on a social media site and, to my surprise, was elated when she was so beautiful. *My kiddos will be gorgeous*, I thought to myself, and I was about to close the lid of my computer when I felt the Lord say, "Look harder." So I obeyed.

I noticed that the picture I was looking at was added while we were in Atlanta, and when I clicked on it, she had a flat belly. My heart sank. I knew at that moment that she was not pregnant but was pretending that she was. Notifying my agency of the information, we began to watch her movements. In the weeks that followed, she gave an excuse for missing every ultrasound opportunity and doctor's appointment.

Eddie and I moved forward with completely pulling out from this birth mom, as there were several reasons why the picture could have looked like she wasn't pregnant. A week after that decision, we received an ultrasound in my email confirming that the woman *was* pregnant with twin girls. I almost fell out of my chair when I looked at it, knowing that this would be a dream come true. We dared to hope that she was pregnant and that these were our babies.

The next morning, the Lord woke me up very early and told me to pray. Sitting in our front room, smelling the pumpkin candle I had lit and drinking coffee before the sun came up brought me a stillness my soul needed. While poring over the pages of Scripture, the Lord seemed to comfort me even though I thought there was no reason for the comfort. Thanking the Lord for His love for me, I concluded my prayer time and got my kiddos off to school.

Later that day, I was on the phone with my brother, explaining to him the confusing ultrasound, and he said, "Have you searched online for fake ultrasounds?" Quickly, I said, "No." We did look at some images, but the ultrasound didn't match any that we saw. As soon as my brother said that, I grabbed my computer and I typed in "fake ultrasounds." The search brought up several sites. I chose one website at random to look at. Still on the phone with my brother, I stopped clicking through the pictures when I saw the same ultrasound picture that had been emailed to us. It was a fake. It was all a lie.

Devastated, I yelled for Eddie, who was on the other side of the house. My heart was racing as I read the details of the site. Personalized, fake sonograms could be purchased for just $24.95. Our dream of twins was over. We had been betrayed and had spent thousands of dollars on what we thought was a promising future.

Let's Get Real

When you are grievously hurt, the idea of forgiving the one who has hurt you makes you want to vomit. The thought of looking that person in the face, the one who knowingly caused you excruciating pain, sickens you. I've been there; I get it. You try to analyze why a person has done what he or she has done to you.

In my world of heartache, I have felt the sting of severe offense. There is no greater pain than when you have been a casualty of someone's betrayal, deceit, anger, abuse or neglect. It is tempting to take on a victim mentality when you have been unjustly treated. However, *you* are not a victim. The victim mentality is a temptation for anyone who has been unjustly treated. Being willing to forgive, and having a right understanding of how to execute forgiveness, will enable you to forgo that line of thinking.

Forgiveness Is Possible When Your Focus Is the Lord

It was difficult to deal with the anger and frustration of finding out that the woman we were emotionally attached to because we thought she was carrying our babies had betrayed us. Especially when we knew she was aware of our desperate desire to adopt. Stealing our money and time and trust sent a shock wave through us. But in the aftermath, forgiveness was our only option. Why? Because I have chosen not to place my eyes on the offender, but on my great Defender. Biblically, God commands us to forgive. He told Peter, as recorded in Matthew 18:21-22, that he was supposed to forgive someone who had wronged him not just seven times, but seventy times seven—a number representing no limit to forgiveness. The Bible also says that God will not hear our prayers if forgiveness is not a part of our lives.

> And when you stand praying, if you hold anything against anyone, forgive him, so that your Father in heaven may forgive you your sins (Mark 11:25, *NIV*).

God was so intentional with these strong statements on forgiveness because He knew the brutal effect of not forgiving others. Anger, bitterness and resentment take up residence in the soul that refuses to live with a forgiving heart. One of the major hindrances to your calling is when you choose not to forgive.

No matter the harm done to you, you must forgive; unforgiveness steals your joy. Constantly clinging to the hurts that have befallen you occupies your mind so heavily that it distracts you from what God may be asking of you. You are not on this planet for you. You are on this planet to accomplish God's plan for you, which revolves around His glory. His glory can only be expressed in you when you forgive others the way He graciously laid down His life and forgave you. Any other thought process is satanic.

Trust me here. I've been hurt so badly emotionally that it hurt me physically. One of the hardest choices to forgive was when my home church, where my dad was the pastor, chose church discipline when I filed for divorce from an abusive man. That in itself could have turned me into an atheist. The abusive marriage, and then being disciplined for getting out of the abuse, could have wrecked my life if I had not chosen to focus on my God.

Forgiveness will be impossible if your focus is not on the Lord. People say, "Forgiveness is a choice," and they are right; but the most important choice, before you forgive, is where you put your focus. If I chose to focus on the things that have happened to me, I would have a hard time with forgiveness; but it is much easier when I turn my attention off of my pain and onto God's plan.

I want to address in more depth the issue of being hurt by the church. I love the local church, and so does God. If Satan can get us to blame all of our reasons why we don't attend church on one individual, or maybe on a few individuals in leadership, he has won.

I know for a fact that there was an attack on me to try to get me to abandon my faith because of the way a church treated me. If I hadn't been focused on the Lord, that attack may have been successful. Church hurts run deep, but not deeper than the healing power of God.

If you have been hurt by the church, do not assume that what happened to you represents all churches. That is a lie from the pit of hell. There are amazing churches out there that are anointed with the power of God, and He wants you to forgive and reengage to benefit you in your relationship with Him. Human beings lead the church, but they don't get it right all the time. I have not been asked by any of the individuals who hurt me at my home church to forgive them, but I have forgiven them, because my focus is the Lord.

Colossians 1:17 says, "He is before all things, and in Him all things hold together." When you have been betrayed, instead of focusing on the betrayal, focus on the One who can hold your future together. We make forgiveness hard by trying to forgive others in our own strength. When we focus on the Lord, the act of forgiving comes naturally.

Forgiving the Unforgivable: Joseph's Story

In Genesis 37, we meet a man by the name of Joseph. Joseph was the son of Jacob and Rachel. He had 11 brothers. For many reasons, Joseph's brothers were very jealous of him. Among the reasons, Joseph's father favored him. Jacob had made Joseph a coat of many colors, which represented Jacob's love for him.

His brothers couldn't handle the favoritism their father showed to Joseph. The Bible says they hated him and couldn't even speak to him on friendly terms (see Gen. 37:4). When Joseph had a couple of dreams that basically were visions of the future, both dreams represented the family bowing down to him. When Joseph told his brothers and father of the dreams, the brothers hated him even more.

Joseph was innocent of any sin against his brothers. It wasn't Joseph's fault that his father showed favoritism or that he had two dreams that were prophetic of the future; but his brothers were so jealous of him that they decided to do the unthinkable: they plotted to get rid of him.

When Jacob sent Joseph to check on his brothers while they were working out in the fields, the brothers seized their chance to get rid of Joseph. First, they were going to kill him. But Reuben, Joseph's eldest brother, talked them out of it. Instead, they stripped him down and ripped the multi-colored coat off of him and threw him into a pit. If you read the text, after they threw him into the pit, the brothers sat down to eat. They were so celebratory from doing so much evil that they had a meal (see Gen. 37:25). While they were eating, there were some Midianite traders that passed by, and the brothers decided to sell Joseph to them for 20 pieces of silver. The brothers hauled Joseph out of the pit and gave him to the traders, who took him to Egypt.

Now, this was a horrible evil done to Joseph, but I'm sure we can relate on some level. Joseph was severely bullied by his brothers, and he was almost killed by those who were closest to him. The hurts done to us by those who are closest to us are the most painful. All of us can relate to a family member hurting us in some way. Imagine the pain Joseph felt as he rode to Egypt with the Midianites. In a whirlwind of events, his bothers abused him, betrayed him and banished him from the father who desperately loved him.

After selling Joseph, they killed a goat, dipped Joseph's coat in its blood and went back to their father and told him a wild animal had attacked Joseph.

There was no "I'm sorry" that was offered to Joseph, or any sort of remorse for their sin against him. It was simply cold-blooded hatred that motivated them. Joseph could have crumbled under this immense offense that was done to him by his siblings, and I'm sure he was tempted to.

When You Have a Dream or Vision for Your Life, Forgiveness Will Be Important

The event that caused Joseph's brothers to act on their resentment was Joseph's dreams. When he dreamed that the family would bow down to him, the jealousy raging in his brothers overcame them. They hated him for what they didn't possess. They hadn't had a dream; they were jealous of Joseph for understanding where God was going to take him.

It is very difficult for people to be wholly supportive of something that is greater than what they see for themselves. Joseph's revelation that one day his brothers would bow down to him was difficult for the brothers to accept. If you are someone with vision for your life, and you know where God is leading you, the need to forgive will become a part of it. People will misinterpret your actions and your words and, at times, they will not understand where God has told you to go, because He didn't tell them. It is your job to live with a forgiving spirit when jealousy, gossip or misunderstanding gets directed toward you. It will happen. Do not get caught up in what someone says or does; that will only sidetrack the vision God has given you.

It's a waste of time to harbor unforgiveness toward people who do not understand what God is asking you to do. When you keep your focus on the Lord and your intent is to do exactly what He wants you to do, He will give you the grace to forgive even when those closest to you hurt you because they misunderstand.

One of the hardest things throughout the 10 years I prayed for The Blush Network was building up enough courage to tell others what God had told me. I used to struggle with what people thought about me. I wanted to be liked, and for sure I didn't want to be laughed at. Even though I knew what God had told me, my circumstances at that time didn't support the vision. I was broke, young, divorced and had absolutely no connections. So the vision of leading a national conference for young women seemed insane.

I remember telling my husband early on about my vision. He looked at me a little strangely, but he responded with immense support, saying, "One day, I am going to sell your books for you at your product table." I will never forget that statement from Eddie. It was confirmation that God was working in him to support me in this vision.

Others were not so supportive when I told them of the vision, and at times my confidence was eclipsed by fear. I knew that outing my dreams would make them subject to scrutiny, but God was clear in telling me to begin sharing, and so I did. I began by telling my parents, who immediately had questions I wasn't prepared to answer. Their how, who, what and why were questions for which I had no answers. All I knew was that God had said it and it was going to happen.

As I began to share with others, I would get a puzzled look each time. A few times, I was accused of not submitting to my husband and not being a "helpmeet." For a while, I was perceived as a controlling wife who was only after what I wanted.

That time in my life was key in developing my confidence in God and not in man. It turned out that I needed people to look at me skeptically, because it drove me to dependence on God's Word. I knew that what I was saying was difficult to believe, and I knew that I might have reacted the same way if someone had said those kinds of things to me. With every criticism, I had to decide to look at the response in a forgiving way, knowing that, in time, God would reveal what He had shown me. Trust me, the negative reactions were incredibly difficult for me, but quitting under the opinion of man was not an option. The vision was clear, and man's response to it was irrelevant.

When Joseph outed his dream to his family, I'm sure his family's questions came as swords to his heart. Even Jacob, his doting father, questioned the dream; but it is evident from the rest of Joseph's story that what he was subjected to developed his dependence on the word of the Lord.

Forgiveness Gets Easier When Injustice Makes Sense

While clinging to the dream, Joseph's problems had just begun. After Joseph was sold to the Midianites, he was then sold as a slave in Egypt to a man by the name of Potiphar, who was an Egyptian officer of Pharaoh's. Joseph found great favor with Potiphar, because Potiphar saw that God walked with Joseph. Potiphar put Joseph in charge of his entire household; and because of Joseph, God blessed the house of Potiphar (see Gen. 39:5).

Then, just as all was going well, Potiphar's wife propositioned him to sleep with her. When Joseph said no, she got angry and lied to her husband, telling him that Joseph had tried to rape her. Joseph was then thrown into prison.

Yet again, Joseph had to bear severe injustice. There he was, sitting in prison while innocent of the charges against him. I'm sure it was hard for Joseph to understand that God was propelling him toward the fulfillment of his prophetic dreams when he had to endure so many wrongs. But that was exactly what God was up to. The dream of Joseph's brothers bowing down to him was in the process of becoming a reality.

Not long after he was thrown in prison, Joseph found favor with the chief jailor, and once again he was put in charge. This time, all the prisoners were under his watch. God prospered Joseph in his circumstances. God had placed Joseph in prison unjustly to do something mighty. The fulfillment of the dream was at stake, and God was on task to accomplish it.

When Pharaoh's cupbearer and baker offended Pharaoh, he threw them in jail. While in jail, they had dreams they wanted interpreted. Joseph was able to interpret the dreams correctly. He asked both men to remember him when they went before Pharaoh, but they forgot. Joseph spent two more years in prison until the day Pharaoh had a dream and demanded it be interpreted. No one could interpret the dream. And then God moved. The cupbearer who had his dream interpreted by Joseph a couple of years before this remembered him and told Pharaoh of Joseph's gift. Joseph's interpretation of Pharaoh's dream was that God was going to give Egypt seven years of plenty followed by seven years of famine.

Standing before Pharaoh was the opportunity God had put in motion way back when Joseph was sold into slavery. Each and every hurt Joseph had endured led him to this one moment. Every lie, every act of betrayal and abuse carried him to the moment when God would carry out the interpretation of his dream.

I remember such a moment in my life. My God-given dream of The Blush Network was yet to be fulfilled when Eddie was laid off from a church in Phoenix. At that time we also faced a horrible court battle brought against us over some extended family issues. Everywhere we turned it seemed that we were being unjustly treated. Then we landed in the office of the pastor of First Baptist Dallas to talk to him about Eddie working as a youth pastor there. As I sat there, I felt like Joseph before Pharaoh. I knew that God could use this man to help me accomplish the dream God had for my life. When I pitched my dream, scared out of my mind, God showed me favor, and that is where I was allowed to begin The Blush Network conference.

When Pharaoh saw that God had given Joseph the wisdom to interpret his dream, he understood that Joseph also had the wisdom to manage the land during the manifestation of the dream. So Joseph became the number-two leader in the nation of Egypt.

The things that have been done to you will benefit you if you turn them over to the power of the Lord. Living a life of bitterness and anger will not set you up for blessing; but living a life that is forgiving, no matter the depth of the hurt, will.

Joseph had two sons, Manasseh, which means "causing me to forget," and Ephraim, which means "fruitful." Joseph named his sons these names because he understood that God had turned his life around for good.

> Joseph named the firstborn Manasseh, "For," he said, "God has made me forget all my trouble and all my father's household." He named the second Ephraim, "For," he said, "God has made me fruitful in the land of my affliction" (Gen. 41:51-52).

The pain and injustice you've endured are part of God's plan to grow you and move you to a place of dream fulfillment. I would not be the person I am today without my trials. The trials I went through because of the actions of others have aided in the vision for my life. Take the betrayal and trials out of my life and I would not be the same person; I wouldn't be as passionate for the Lord or as resolute in doing exactly what He wants for my life. Understanding this makes me want to forgive.

Look at Jesus: While unjustly hanging on the cross, He asked God to forgive the ones who crucified Him.

But Jesus was saying, "Father, forgive them; for they do not know what they are doing" (Luke 23:34).

Jesus knew that every piece of pain He was going through unjustly was achieving salvation for mankind. He wasn't focused on the injustice, because it produced God's perfect will. When you have this perspective, you are in the center of God's will. He will always use your pain to accomplish something greater.

Forgiveness Fulfills the Promise

Because of the horrific famine in the land, Joseph's brothers needed to go to Egypt to buy food, which meant they had to go before Joseph, who was second in command in Egypt. Joseph finally came face to face with the men who had sold him to the Midianites and had convinced his father that he was dead. The time for the fulfillment of the dream had come. His brothers did bow down to him. This stirred enormous emotion in Joseph. He disguised himself for a time, but when the time came to reveal himself to his brothers, he wept.

He wept so loudly that the Egyptians heard it, and the household of Pharaoh heard of it (Gen. 45:2).

At this point, Joseph knew why he had been mistreated. It was clear by his emotion that he had forgiven his brothers and was moved to see them. When he revealed himself to them, they freaked out because they all knew the horrible injustice they had done to him, and he had the power to have them put to death. But Joseph answered them kindly:

Now do not be grieved or angry with yourselves, because you sold me here, for God sent me before you to preserve life (Gen. 45:5).

All of the injustice Joseph went through led up to this moment. God had sent him there and moved through the injustice.

Now, therefore, it was not you who sent me here, but
God; and He has made me a father to Pharaoh and lord
of all his household and ruler over all the land of Egypt
(Gen. 45:8).

Please stay with me on this. Jacob, Joseph's father's name,
was changed to Israel. He had 12 sons who began the 12 tribes
of the nation of Israel—God's chosen people. Israel is the nation that brought forth God's Son, Jesus. God chose Joseph to
foreshadow our Savior, Jesus Christ. Joseph's forgiveness of his
brothers was part of the fulfillment of the promise God gave
to Abraham in Genesis 12. Joseph could have killed all of his
brothers in retribution for what they did to him, but he chose
to forgive them, making it possible for you and me to be forgiven of our sins through Jesus Christ, whose lineage was the
nation of Israel.

Understand, this was the act of forgiveness that enabled a
nation of people to benefit. If Joseph had not chosen to forgive
them, the very nation of Israel that was promised to Abraham,
Isaac and Jacob would have been silenced. Another name for
Jesus is Lion of the Tribe of Judah; and one of Joseph's brother's
names was Judah.

I know that was deep, but the takeaway is that by choosing
to not forgive those who have hurt you in the past, you could
rob yourself of what God wants to do through your forgiving
heart. Who knows how He has knit your life together and what
He has planned? Your significance will require you to forgive; by
doing so, you enable God to do wonders through you. It blows
my mind that Joseph saved the nation of Israel because of his
act of forgiveness. What could God be waiting to do in your life,
but lack of forgiveness is hindering it?

You Don't Need an Apology to Forgive

I don't know what has been done against you, but I do know
this: No pain is wasted. All pain is for your benefit. Holding on
to offense and deciding not to forgive someone results in your
forgoing the benefit of God's plan. What people mean for evil,

God always means for good. And when He is your focus, forgiveness isn't difficult.

There is no injustice so horrific that God cannot turn it around for the amazement of all. Let it go, sweet friend. As hard as it may be, you don't need an apology in order to forgive; you need a new perspective. Apologies have nothing to do with forgiveness. But Joseph's brothers were finally compelled to ask for Joseph's forgiveness:

> Thus you shall say to Joseph, "Please forgive, I beg you, the transgression of your brothers and their sin, for they did you wrong. And now, please forgive the transgression of the servants of the God of your father." And Joseph wept when they spoke to him. Then his brothers also came and fell down before him and said, "Behold we are your servants" (Gen. 50:17-18).

Finally, Joseph saw the true fulfillment of the dream he had revealed so many years before of his brothers bowing down before him and telling him that they were his servants. Joseph readily forgave his brothers. His response was amazing:

> As for you, you meant evil against me, but God meant it for good in order to bring about this present result, to preserve many people alive (Gen. 50:20).

Most times in my life when I have needed to forgive, I have not received an apology. Sweet reader, I adore you, but please don't wait for an apology. Understand that the opportunity to forgive will have a huge effect on the significance of your calling. Choose today to forgive, no matter the offense, and let God deal with the consequences.

QUESTIONS THAT SEEK TRUTH

1. Debilitating hurt makes forgiveness of the offense difficult. Why is this so?
2. When you have a God-given dream or vision for your life, forgiveness will be a part of it. Do you have a dream for your life? What is it?

3. Have you experienced jealousy, misunderstanding or discouragement from others while interpreting that dream?

4. The wrongs done to Joseph actually propelled him toward his calling. It was because of what was done to him that Joseph was able to achieve his calling. How have the wrongs done to you aided you in your calling?

5. Are you at a place where you can forgive? How has reading this chapter moved you in that direction?

6. Without Joseph's forgiveness of his brothers, the very nation of Israel would not exist. What could your refusal to forgive be costing the world?

7. Do you need an apology in order to forgive someone who has done you wrong?

8. Even if you never receive an apology, can you see why it is essential for you to forgive?

9. It's easier to forgive when you let yourself grieve the offense. Have you allowed yourself to grieve the emotions associated with the offense in order to surrender them and forgive?

10. Who have you yet to forgive? Spend time in prayer and ask God to help you take care of that.

12

The Significance of Your Future

I definitely struggle with remembering that I am significant.

BLUSH ATTENDEE

What is keeping you from God's vision for your life?

If you have ever believed that you are not a visionary, I beg to differ with you. I have been confronted many times on the issue of vision, and usually the first line of out of the individual's mouth is, "I don't have the gift of vision." This is problematic thinking. If a person knows that God has a plan for his or her life, wouldn't you agree that the plan could also be called a *vision* for his or her life?

People who think that just because they are not Walt Disney or Steve Jobs that means they are not visionaries and that they are living completely boring lives.

What we think determines our actions. Not believing you could be a person of vision will therefore subtract visions from your life. If I believed that I didn't have a gift of speaking, I wouldn't be a speaker. I would literally not think thoughts of desiring to speak on a stage. I would focus on what I did believe.

I want to challenge your way of thinking. I believe that you can be a visionary for your own life. If you believe that God has a vision, a plan, for your life, then you automatically have vision. Your job is to seek what the vision is and follow after it. If you are lazy and do not take the time to seek, you will miss out. Vision unrealized is vision lost.

After praying for eight years about The Blush Network, before God had given me the opportunity to launch it, I began to feel a quickening in my spirit. I knew at any time that I could expect the Lord to open the door for the conference ministry He had shown me. I began intentionally praying about it. Wisdom, resources, strength and support were all things that were heavy in my prayers. Without the direct ask from the Lord to start the conference ministry, I would never have considered it. Even though the task seemed insurmountable for a small-town, broke girl, God thought it fit me perfectly. Prayer and faith that God could achieve the impossible and improbable fueled my hope.

In 2009, not yet knowing how the conference ministry would launch, I felt a conviction that it was time to name the ministry. I had prayed for years, not knowing exactly what God wanted for the name. I knew that I didn't want the name to be too churchy. I wanted it to attract those who were not familiar with church. But I also wanted it to be feminine. "The Blush Network" worked on both accounts. Just a few months after God had given me the name, He gave me the opportunity to launch the ministry. He alerted me that the timing was near and to get things in order so that He could fulfill the promise He had given me years earlier.

I have to be honest and tell you I received flack for adding "The" and "Network" to the name. Many people's opinions were to just name the ministry Blush. However, I knew that even though God had called me to a conference ministry, He wanted to do more with whatever platform He would give us. We would start with conferences, and God would reveal when the timing was right to expand. I wanted to create a network for women, not just a one-time event. The vision for the ministry has played out just as God told me it would with the expansion to Latina conferences, small groups, an intern program, leadership programming and one-night events.

Let's Get Real

The Wasteland of Vision

There is a barren wasteland in the Christian culture that is populated with the unfulfilled visions for individuals' lives. In that wasteland you can see God-given jobs and tasks that were to be completed for His glory, yet were passed over and substituted with living a life of "happiness." Satanic and fleshly influences have talked droves of people into bypassing what God wants them to do because the journey is too hard and the path is too narrow. I weep for these people. They are saturated with intellectual knowledge about our most amazing God, but they are not able, for one reason or another, to perform for Him. They have abandoned the fullness of their inheritance. They live by an anthem of excuses. They have bypassed the vision God created solely for them in their time to achieve fulfillment, and thereby have passed up the opportunity to give glory to our amazing God.

I shudder when I think of how this described seven years of my life. I chose my own way and married a man who was not in line with God's plans for me. I could have been steadily working for my King during this time, but I trashed those seven years instead, and they reside in the wasteland of vision. I used every excuse, insecurity and circumstance to override what I knew God wanted to accomplish in me. In taking my life into my own hands, I almost ruined it.

If you read through the Scriptures, you will see that people who were given a vision and a commission from the Lord always had a reason why they shouldn't be the one God was choosing. When Isaiah was given the vision of the Lord seated on His throne, the vision of God immediately convicted him of his sin and inadequacy before the Lord: "Then I said, 'Woe is me, for I am ruined! Because I am a man of unclean lips, and I live among a people of unclean lips; for my eyes have seen the King, the LORD of hosts'" (Isa. 6:5). Do you think God was intimidated by Isaiah's mouth? No! God immediately prepared Isaiah for his commission (see Isa. 6:7). God chose Isaiah to be His mouthpiece to the nation of Israel. The Lord quickly resolved Isaiah's excuse of why he shouldn't be chosen, and then He commissioned him.

Isaiah didn't let his inadequacy interfere with his opportunity, and neither should you. You only have a limited lifespan on this planet; it would be a travesty if you gave up all your opportunities in the future because of insecurity. Choosing to do nothing with your life is much easier than choosing to live out God's vision to the fullest, but oh what you would give up to make that choice! Don't live in the wasteland.

When God gave Jeremiah the commission for his life, He began the commission with these words:

> Before I formed you in the womb I knew you, and before you were born I consecrated you; I have appointed you a prophet to the nations (Jer. 1:5).

The text explains that before Jeremiah was even formed, God appointed Jeremiah to represent Him. The traits God gave Jeremiah were to fulfill his calling as a prophet to the nations. Note Jeremiah's response:

> Then I said, "Alas, Lord GOD! Behold, I do not know how to speak, because I am a youth" (Jer. 1:6).

Right after God's amazing statement that Jeremiah was fashioned to be a prophet to the nations, Jeremiah refutes the calling with the excuse that he is too young. When we are called to do something for the Lord, it will be outside of our comfort zone. Jeremiah was just like you and me in his concern that he wasn't good enough to accomplish being a mouthpiece to the nations. However, in the end, he didn't let that sway him to give over his life to the wasteland.

God is so good to us that He answers our insecurities just as He answered Jeremiah's in the very next verses:

> But the Lord said to me, "Do not say, 'I am a youth.' Because everywhere I send you, you shall go, and all that I command you, you shall speak. Do not be afraid of them, for I am with you to deliver you," declares the LORD (Jer. 1:7-8).

God created your weaknesses and your strengths and He fashioned them in such a way that you will not be hindered, as you live in His power, from accomplishing what He wants you to accomplish as long as it is subjected and surrendered to Him.

Godly Vision Never Originates with You; It Originates with God

Don't get it twisted, my sweet reader; God is the one who creates and distributes vision. Every day I come in contact with people who are almost obsessed with their wants and desires and dreams for their life. If God has not given you the plan for your life, these dreams, hopes and desires are meaningless.

The *only* way to achieve your significance is to focus solely on the Lord. You were created and crafted specifically for God's vision for your life, not your own. Your plan for your life when compared with God's plan for you would embarrass you. I hear people say, "I just want to be happy," so they seek what they think will make them happy. When the "thing" is achieved, they find themselves just as unhappy as they were before. Human perspective is small-minded and futile. Yet, we believe that we can achieve happiness for ourselves. Hear me: *Happiness should never be our goal.*

I will never desire for my children to be happy. I do, however, desperately desire them to be fulfilled in the calling the Lord has placed them on this earth to achieve. I know that in doing so they will achieve contentment and joy.

The life of the apostle Paul is a great example of what could be achieved when he finally focused only on what God had called him to do. Before that, Paul's plan for his life was to be one of the main instigators in the great persecution of the church in Jerusalem. In Acts 8:3, the Bible says that he ravaged the church, entering house after house and dragging off men and women to put them in prison for believing in Jesus. I assume this is what he wanted to do with his life. His intent was to protect the sacred way of the law, not realizing that the world now lived under the great grace of God. Paul's plan for his life as he carried it out was embarrassing compared to what God had created him to achieve.

God's vision for Paul's life was that he would be the first and the most effective missionary to proclaim the gospel of Jesus Christ to the Gentiles (that's us) as well as to Jews, and it didn't start until God spoke to him and blinded him on the road to Damascus (you can read the story in Acts 9). The Lord called Paul a "chosen instrument." If Paul had not heeded the call of the Lord and changed his direction, we would not have most of the New Testament. God crafted Paul for something much greater than he could ever imagine; but he had to hear from the Lord to achieve it. After Paul heard from the Lord, happiness was not even a thought; his only desire was to bring God glory through God's vision for his life.

Your Vision Meets a Unique Need

God's vision for all of us is that our lives will meet needs in the world. There is no need for which God doesn't have an answer. The biblical heroes of the faith were normal men and women like us who answered a need by acting on God's vision for their lives. In our flesh, we think that God doesn't want to use us, but that is completely contrary to His way. He created us for His use.

Let's look at God's call to Moses. When Moses was pasturing the flock of his father-in-law, the angel of the Lord appeared to him in a burning bush.

> When the LORD saw that he turned aside to look, God called to him from the midst of the bush and said, "Moses, Moses!" He said, "Here I am" (Exod. 3:4).

I love that God didn't speak to Moses until Moses turned and looked. To be called and shown the vision for our lives, we must be looking for it. A deliberate action took place on Moses' part—the action of looking. When we choose to look to the Lord, He will begin to speak. God speaks when He has our attention. He is aware of when He has our utmost attention and we will hear Him. The vision for Moses' life was given to him when he turned his attention to the Lord. His answer was, "Here I am."

God was literally waiting for Moses to turn and look at the burning bush. Moses wasn't seeking the Lord, but he encountered Him when he paid attention. We all have opportunity for the burning bush experience. God is waiting, sweet reader, to reveal His plan for your future. The bush is burning, and He waits patiently for you to drop your distractions and turn your attention to Him. Direction from the Lord begins with your action.

God had already decided what Moses was going to do. There was a huge need in the land of Egypt; the Israelites needed a leader to bring them out of their bondage. Moses' vision for his life was not up for discussion. God had created him for that purpose.

Therefore, come now, and I will send you to Pharaoh, so that you may bring My people, the sons of Israel, out of Egypt (Exod. 3:10).

Notice in this verse that the Lord didn't ask for Moses' opinion. God stated the need and then gave the vision and mission for Moses' life. God isn't interested in your opinion; He wants your obedience. God had created Moses to meet the need of His chosen people. Moses rebutted with the words, "Who am I, that I should go to Pharaoh, and that I should bring the sons of Israel out of Egypt?" (Exod. 3:11). God comforted Him immediately by saying, "Certainly I will be with you" (Exod. 3:12). It is ridiculous to tell God that you are incapable of the vision for your life. You simply need to accept it and know that God will certainly be with you to help you achieve it.

From Moses' response, we can see that if God hadn't commissioned him to lead the nation of Israel, he would never have done so and would not even have thought of it. He may have known of the need of the people of Israel, but he would not have thought of himself as their leader. Only because God called and commissioned him did Moses act on it.

There is no way I would be doing what I am doing without the Lord asking me to do it. It's too tough and too scary. In my burning bush moment, I responded much like Moses, because I almost couldn't believe that God had such a plan for my life. I am not confident in my own gifts and abilities; I am confident in God alone and His vision for my life. Every time I have felt like giving in, God's power has intervened. I have held to His words, "Certainly I will be with you." I have begged for God to go before me and come behind me every step of the way. And He has never let me down.

The greatest part of what God has called me to do is to take a front-row seat to see spiritual needs met. I have seen countless salvations, decisions to walk away from lifelong sin, and calls to ministry—all because I obeyed. That alone is worth every hardship that has come my way.

God doesn't hand you vision for your life without fully intending that you will fulfill it. With Him, you cannot fail. Seize the vision, sweet reader.

Don't Duplicate What You Were Made to Originate

I fear that we have gotten into the habit of wanting to do something simply because someone else is doing it and has had success at it. I have had the opportunity to speak all over the country, and I often hear, "I want to do what you do." My first question is, "Why?"

It's possible that you can be passionate about a type of venture yet it is not the vision God has for your life. A word of caution: Don't seek your passion in order to determine God's call for your life; seek God directly. Passion is fleeting. You may be passionate one day about something and two weeks later forget what that thing is. I believe that passion is an amazing trait. I certainly don't want to discourage it! However, passion will fade away when tough times come.

God wants you to carry out your original vision—the one He crafted you for. Seeking Him is the only way to do that. He will not allow you to share someone else's vision. Your vision is unique to you. I get concerned when I hear that someone wants to do exactly what someone else is doing, because I know that God's vision for his or her life is not a duplication of someone else's. It may have some of the same characteristics, but it will never duplicate it. Duplicating someone else's vision is a good way to slap God in the face. If you try to copy someone else's dreams or visions, you will be frustrated and waste time that you could have spent on what God wants you to do. God's vision for your life will be just as thrilling to you as theirs is to them.

In 1 Samuel 17, we see that young David was told by his father to take food and supplies to his brothers as they waited to fight the Philistines. When David arrived on the scene to deliver the goods, he saw that there was a giant named Goliath who was taunting the army of the nation of Israel. Goliath, as you may have heard, was enormously big and tall—a champion amongst the Philistine army. For this particular battle, the plan for combat was to pit champion against champion. The entire army was not involved; one champion from the Philistines would fight one champion from Israel, and whoever won would win the battle.

The stakes were high for the combatant for Israel. The odds of winning over a guy like Goliath were slim to none; he would not only lose the battle for Israel, but also he would lose his life.

For 40 days, Goliath taunted the nation of Israel, and not one man was courageous enough to fight him. Not one of the thousands who waited there understood that they were in the army of the nation of God's chosen people. Not one believed that the God who had parted the Red Sea was in their midst. Not one trusted that the hand of the Lord was with them. That is, until the boy David showed up.

All of the soldiers turned in fear and chose to forget the divine power that was accessible to them. When David saw the depth of despair that had fallen on the army, his response was unparalleled:

> For who is this uncircumcised Philistine, that he should taunt the armies of the living God? (1 Sam. 17:26).

David chose to fight the great Goliath because no one else would. It wasn't the popular choice; it wasn't recommended; but it was the choice that caused the Philistines to be defeated. As David approached Goliath to fight him, his words were direct:

> Then David said to the Philistine, "You come to me with a sword, spear and javelin, but I come to you in the name of the LORD of hosts, the God of the armies of Israel, whom you have taunted" (1 Sam. 17:45).

David boldly proclaimed that with the LORD of hosts, he would be victorious. He accepted the challenge of a mission that was unique to him, and with one stone in a slingshot, he killed the great Goliath of Gath. David's mission was unpopular, but it was critical.

Our culture screams with many Goliaths taunting our faith. Unborn babies are killed in the name of convenience. Our youth are plagued with images that tempt them to live a life of wickedness. Women are being sold and raped for the sex pleasure of perverts. Pornography is stealing the integrity and purity of men and women who watch in secret. Satan taunts minds into justifying suicide. Our schools are no longer safe.

The world needs you to stand boldly and take up the Goliath that God has asked you to kill. You fight on the side of the living God. He waits for you to take your unique charge and boldly accept His unique vision for your life. Remember, there was only one Moses, one Joshua, one Elijah, one David, one Esther, one Solomon, one Daniel, one Joseph, one Peter, one James and one John. All of these people had high callings, but all were different. There is also only one Jesus. And there is only one you.

Act on the Vision

When I get to heaven, I want to hear God say, "Well done, Autumn Miles." In order to hear those words, I must act on the vision God has for my life.

How about you? The time to act is not in two weeks or after the weekend. The time is right now. God is waiting to use you for His glory in the most beautiful capacity. Your inadequacies don't matter; He simply sees a vision for your life that He planned for you to accept. No matter the pain, the mistakes, the problems or the trials you have experienced, He still wants to use you now.

You are appointed, and the depth of fulfillment you will get from surrendering to His way will blow your mind. Odds are good that He has already been speaking to you and asking you to trust Him. Do it. He is ever trustworthy and will not allow you to be put to shame. Every seemingly shameful moment I have had on my journey with the Lord He has changed into blessing. The vision for your life is not too hard, because God is the God of the impossible.

And looking at them Jesus said to them, "With people this is impossible, but with God all things are possible" (Matt. 19:26).

Is anything too difficult for the LORD? (Gen. 18:14).

I know that You can do all things, and that no purpose of Yours can be thwarted (Job 42:2).

Ah Lord GOD! Behold, You have made the heavens and the earth by Your great power and by Your outstretched arm! Nothing is too difficult for You (Jer. 32:17).

Behold, I am the LORD, the God of all flesh; is anything too difficult for Me? (Jer. 32:27).

And Jesus said to him, "'If You can?' All things are possible to him who believes" (Mark 9:23).

Looking at them, Jesus said, "With people it is impossible, but not with God; for all things are possible with God" (Mark 10:27).

For nothing will be impossible with God (Luke 1:37).

But He said, "The things that are impossible with people are possible with God" (Luke 18:27).

And being fully assured that what God had promised, He was able to perform (Rom. 4:21).

He is able, sweet reader. Don't doubt it. Run to the mighty Author of your life and act on the vision created for you before you were formed. His power will be your strength.

QUESTIONS THAT SEEK TRUTH

1. Do you believe that you are a person of vision? Why, or why not?
2. Do you know someone who has wasted his or her life? What do you think that person abandoned to the wasteland of vision?
3. Any one of us can start living in the wasteland of vision if we are not intentional about our call. What excuse have you used to justify not doing something God wants you to do?
4. The vision for your life never originates with you. It is always God's idea. Have you ever acted out on your desires and forsaken God's desires for you? What are your thoughts about that possibility?

5. It was when Moses turned his head to look at the fire in the bush that God spoke to him about his future. Have you been seeking God for the details of your future?

6. The bush is burning in your life; it has been burning since you were created. Has God revealed something already that He wants you to do? What is it?

7. Your calling has already been decided; that calling is best for you, despite what you may think. Just as God didn't ask for Moses' opinion, so too He doesn't ask for yours. He only asks for your obedience. Are you willing?

8. You were not made to copy someone else's calling; your calling is unique to you. What is God asking you specifically to contribute to?

9. When the vision for your life is revealed, you must act. What first step can you take today to move toward the vision for your life?

10. There is nothing too difficult for the Lord. God can and will help you to achieve your calling. Are you determined to attain it?

Acknowledgments

There has been nothing greater in my life than the grace given to me by my Lord and Savior, Jesus Christ. My God represents my everything. I have nothing to say of worth apart from my God. He has been and will forever be the driving force behind my life. If it wasn't for Him pulling me out of my pit of sin, I would still live in bondage. Deciding to accept the forgiveness found in Him was the most powerful decision I have ever made. His sacrifice for me astounds me.

Apart from my Jesus, by God's grace, He allowed me to marry a man who is 100 percent supportive of God's calling on my life. Eddie Miles's support, since the day we met, has never changed, and he is my biggest cheerleader. Thank you, my dear husband, for continually telling me, "You can do it." I love you.

To my children, Grace and Jude Miles, whose lives have forever changed my perspective on mine: I would not be the person I am today without you. You are both the funniest people I know. Your perspective on life and your thought processes are treasures that I hide deep in my heart. I don't deserve the blessing of being your mom, but I will be forever grateful for the gift.

To my parents, Paul and Sharon Carey: I give great admiration and respect. Without your prayers and your godly example of what faith looks like, my life would look much different today. Thank you both for being giants for our Lord; no matter the circumstances you found yourself in, you always directed me to the Lord. Your support through the darkest time in my life will be support that I will appreciate to the day of my death. No words can express the gratitude I have for you, my parents, in choosing to support me when it wasn't the popular choice. I love you both.

To my brother, David, my sister, Heather, and my sweet sister-in-law, Amanda: I have grown so much as a woman by having godly siblings who speak into my life. Thank you for your passion for the Lord and your utmost determination to have Him be King in your own lives. I do not take lightly the wealth you have given me in love and support. I hope I am half the sibling to you that you have been to me.

To my amazing staff at The Blush Network: I adore each of you. You have taken the vision and made it your own. As we walk down this road of reaching the world with the power that is found in the name of Jesus, I would have no one other than all of you to fight with me. With God by our side, we are victorious. He has never, and will never, let us down. Each of you and your families have sacrificed so much, and I thank you. Servant leadership is found in each of you, and I am proud to have the privilege of ministering with you. You inspire me. Thank you for all you do.

SCRIPTURE INDEX

About Autumn Miles

Autumn Miles was born in Lynchburg, Virginia. She was raised in a small town in Indiana as a pastor's daughter. At age 11, on Easter Sunday, she came to know Christ as her personal Savior (April 12, 1992). After taking a couple of detours spiritually, she came to a point in life when she was desperate for God and, at 21, surrendered her will to Him. Following God's leading, Autumn has completely surrendered to ministering to young women. For three years she taught and led a program called Creative Positive Relationships until she was called to attend Liberty University. Autumn became the first female ministry intern sent out by the university. During this time, she traveled with a ministry team called True Identity where she shared her story of God's faithfulness.

Autumn is a passionate, direct communicator who has spoken at women's events for over fifteen years. She has had the privilege to minister through Liberty University, First Baptist Dallas, Go Tell Ministries' young women's conferences, Shepherd Church Porter Ranch, Care Net, and Cornerstone Church in Chandler, Arizona.

Autumn founded The Blush Network, a women's ministry for which she serves as president. She and her team travel the country, partnering with organizations such as I Am Second, Liberty University and Big Brothers Big Sisters, teaching the women of today about issues of the heart. The Blush Network has launched a student ministry team (Blush ID), a leadership program, an internship program, small groups and a cross-cultural ministry.

Autumn also writes a blog that averages 2,000 readers a month. Autumn published a young women's devotional in 2010 on faith that has been read by women all over the country. She is currently the female lead for Connect 360 in Dallas and co-host of *Power Talk* on 89.7 Power FM.

Aside from her passion for God and ministry, her joy is her family. Autumn married Eddie Miles in 2004 and has two beautiful children—her daughter has a vivacious personality and her son can sweep the world off its feet with his smile.

Spiritually challenging the way women think.

The Blush Network is a national ministry for women whose mission is to spiritually challenge the way women think. We accomplish this through conferences, speaking, leadership training, women's ministry internship programs, cross-cultural ministry, one night events, social media and blogs.

The Blush Network reaches everyone from churched women who want to grow closer to Christ, to homeless women in great need. The Blush Network sees real life change in the areas of abuse, self harm, sexual relationships, salvation, relationship with God, vision, purpose and significance.

What people are saying about The Blush Network

Recently we have been challenging our church body to reach out to our city. Blush came to Columbus and not only ministered to our people but invited women from all around the city to the conference. Blush showed us the needs of not only our church, but the city.
Life Church Gahanna, Ohio

It was such an honor to be part of The Blush Network Latina Edition Conference in Phoenix. The girls I met were such an inspiration and a blessing to my life and I can't wait to be a part of Blush again soon!
Myrka Dellanos

Women who had plans for abortions left the conference with changed hearts and a child to nurture. Women who carried the guilt or embarrassment of previous situations of abuse left with freedom. Women who had no hope when they walked into that building left with a future in Christ. At the end of the day, I was in tears just thinking about how much God cares about us and how all it takes is one moment of submission to have your life changed forever.
Jesse, conference attendee

To Learn More About The Blush Network:
www.theblushnetwork.com Facebook.com/theblushnetwork
Twitter - @blushnetwork

Your Guide to Happily Ever After

The Cinderella Rule
Bethany Jett

Of all the fairytale princesses we know and love, Cinderella is the one who got it right. She knew the spell was about to break, and ran out of the castle just in time to keep her mysterious identity a secret. Prince Charming couldn't help himself! He had to pursue her, to track her down and invite her to be his queen. *The Cinderella Rule* is your guide to letting your prince do the work. Whether he knows it or not, the man God has for you longs to experience the thrill of the chase . . . and that means running out of the castle before you give away all your secrets! Find out how to be a woman of mystery who lets herself be pursued, knowing you are worth every ounce of effort. *The Cinderella Rule* will show you how to be the queen your prince is already looking for.

Learn How to Make the Most of Your Twenties...and Beyond

Beauty, finances, health and relationships are just some of the areas those of us in our twenties and thirties navigate on a daily basis. Many of us know these topics are important, but we feel unprepared to make the critical choices expected of us.

In *Survival Guide for Young Women*, Holly Wagner and Nicole Reyes share biblical wisdom and their personal experiences as they give tips for celebrating your style, managing your wallets, discovering your God-given purpose, and finding healthy friendships. You'll discover the authors' useful how-tos on a wide range of topics—such as smart, godly dating; ways to resolve conflict; and how to buy the right jeans—and you'll have a few laughs along the way! Holly and Nicole also remind us that we don't have to face these (or other) issues on our own. We need each other's wisdom and experiences. We need friends who can encourage us to become more like Jesus and enjoy the abundant life He has for us.

The Survival Guide for Young Women
Holly Wagner & Nicole Reyes

> "*Survival Guide for Young Women* spoke directly to my heart. I cannot think of two better women to share their hearts and insights with us—you will love it!"
> - Kari Jobe, Worship Artist

Available wherever books are sold!